The Diaries of

Dean Charles Fyvie

for 1829 and 1839–1841

Text in this form:
© Diocese of Moray, Ross and Caithness
of the Scottish Episcopal Church,
2013

First published in this form 2013

Published jointly by
Diocese of Moray, Ross and Caithness
(Scottish Charity No. SC004655)
http://www.moray.anglican.org/
and
For the Right Reasons, Inverness
(Scottish Charity No. SC037781)
http://fortherightreasons.net/

ISBN: 978-1-905787-89-0

Printing and binding by
For the Right Reasons,
Printers and Publishers,
60 Grant Street,
Inverness, IV3 8BN

The Diaries of

Very Rev. Charles Fyvie

Minister of St. John's Episcopal Church, Inverness
1819–1849

Dean of the Diocese of Moray
in the Scottish Episcopal Church
1839–1849

covering the years

1829 and 1839–1841

Edited by Robert Preece,

using in part the 1922 edition of

extracts of Dean Fyvie's diary,

edited by an unknown hand

EPISCOPAL CHAPEL INVERNESS.

Design for finishing the Tower by Mackenzie & Matthews, Arch.ts

Index

Illustrations

Acknowledgements:

The Right Rev. Mark J. Strange, Bishop of Moray, Ross and Caithness, for comments on the content.

Donald Preece, for proof-reading and comments.

Source of illustrations:

Exterior of Chapel: from an original in the archives of the Diocese of Moray, Ross and Caithness.

Interior of Chapel: image courtesy *High Life Highland.*

Bishop Alexander Jolly: copied from an engraving by W. H. Lizars in 1840 from an original picture by J. Moir (1821), as used in a 19th-century edition of Bishop Jolly's works *(Observations on Sunday Services; etc.).*

Bishop Andrew Macfarlane: from a silhouette portrait in the possession of the Diocese of Moray, Ross and Caithness, image courtesy of *Am Baile (High Life Highland).*

Bishop David Low: from a portrait in the possession of the Diocese of Argyll and the Isles.

Rev. Aberigh-Mackay: image courtesy of *Am Baile (High Life Highland)*, originally from *Sutherland and the Reay Country*, edited by Rev. Adam Gunn and John Mackay, 1897.

The graves of Dean Fyvie and Rev. James Hay: photo by the present editor.

Duffus Chapel and Manse: from a photocopy in the Diocesan archive taken from an unidentified book, copyright owner not established.

THE DIARIES OF DEAN CHARLES FYVIE

Foreword

The volume containing the diaries of Dean Charles Fyvie has lain in the archive of St. John's Scottish Episcopal Church in Southside Road, Inverness, for many years.[1] Extensive extracts from these diaries were published by Robt. Carruthers & Sons, Inverness, probably in late 1922, using material printed in the *Inverness Courier* in June of that year. However that edition has long since been almost unavailable.

The previously published extracts included comments by an unknown editor providing information about Dean Fyvie and St. John's Church, and setting the diaries in the context of the time. As a document of social history, as well as for its ecclesiastical outlook, it is now time for a further issue. The diary for the years 1839 to 1841 also provides a detailed weather diary, to set alongside some other similar documents known to survive from the first half of the nineteenth century.

The diaries are handwritten in a hard-backed notebook, which is in poor condition, with the first 26 pages missing. A bad repair has reattached the front cover to the remaining pages, but the back cover and the last few pages are loose. The cover itself has a large typescript label saying:

Presented to
S. John's Church
Inverness
by
Mr. Hugh Mackenzie
Tain Cottage
Fairfield Road
Inverness

but there is no date given for the presentation.

Like many similar documents from the early part of the 19th century, the punctuation and spelling in the original diaries are somewhat variable in style, and this has been edited here so as to be easier for the modern reader to follow. Also, the style of the Biblical references has been standardised, as they too are somewhat variable in the original. Place names and people's names have generally been transcribed as written, but 'Rose-heath', 'Rose Heath' and

[1] National Register of Archives of Scotland (NRAS): Ref. NRAS4317/1/19/5/1

'Roseheath', Dean Fyvie's house, have been standardised into the last of the three versions. 'Muirton' and 'Muirtown' are also used interchangeably, and have been standardised here to the second version. Some phrases that might be seen today as grammatically wrong have not be changed.

Dean Fyvie also often abbreviated common words like 'Christ', 'the' and 'and': these have generally here been rendered in full. Some of his underlining of key words has been omitted in this edition where such a device would not be used today; it has been retained where relevant.

A few words have defied transcription and these are shown by 'xxxxx'. A few doubtful transcriptions are indicated by *[?]* after the word in question. There are also a number of '† day' or '+ day' notes at the end of certain entries – these seem to imply a difficult day, one when Dean Fyvie "had a cross to bear".

Editorial comment from the 1922 edition of the diary has been reproduced in full (pages 11-13, 22-23 and 113-114), although some errors have been corrected. Insertions into the original text are shown in italic type, to explain matters which might not be understood by the modern reader, and to provide biographical notes about many of the people mentioned. Those notes in square brackets have been provided by the present editor; those in curved brackets by the editor of the 1922 edition of the diaries. Some illustrations have also been provided in this edition, but no portrait of Dean Fyvie has been identified.

Dean Fyvie published a booklet of psalms and hymns, dedicated to the members of his Inverness congregation. The title page is missing from the only known copy,[2] and no publication date is given. The National Library of Scotland also has a copy of a sermon, published in 1823, entitled *The Duties and Difficulties of the Christian Ministry*. Some handwritten sermons almost certainly by Fyvie, dated from 1817 to 1828, are held in the Diocesan archive.[3]

The clergy of St. John's Chapel/Church from 1688 (the time of the abolition of the episcopacy in the Established Church in Scotland) until the 1850's were:

> Hector Mackenzie (1688–1719)
> Robert Jameson (1719–1734)
> James Hay (1734–1758)
> John Stewart (1759–1770)
> William Mackenzie (1770)
> *Charge served from Arpafeelie in the Black Isle until 1779*
> Andrew Macfarlane (1779–1819)

[2] Ref. NRAS4317/1/19/5/3

[3] Ref. NRAS4318/7/3

Charles Fyvie (1819–1849)
James Aberigh-Mackay (1849–1857)

The Bishops of Moray shortly before and around the time that Charles Fyvie was incumbent at St. John's were:

Andrew Macfarlane (1787–1798)
Alexander Jolly (1798–1838)
David Low (1838–1850)

and the Bishops of Ross were:

Andrew Macfarlane (1798–1819)
David Low (1819–1850)

The Diocese were linked in various ways in the nineteenth century, with Moray and Ross generally joined, sometimes with Argyle (as it was then spelled), and from 1864 with Caithness. The Diocese of Moray extends right along the coast of the Moray Firth as far as Banff. Argyll (with the Isles) became a diocese in its own right in 1847.

To gain some idea of local events, including the considerable controversy within the Church of Scotland at the time (which would lead to the Disruption of 1843), see *The Northern Highlands in the Nineteenth Century*, compiled from the files of the *Inverness Courier* of the time by James Barron, and published from 1907. Volume 2 covers the relevant years. It is easily consulted through the Highland Library Service's reference rooms, and is now available on-line.

For a view on the local social conditions and norms of the middle class of the time, see Isabel Anderson's *Inverness before Railways*, first published in 1885. This explains that dinner in the early nineteenth century was normally served at 4 p.m., sometimes later if there was to be a party. Young unmarried people were not often asked to attend dinner, but invited for tea afterwards, at perhaps 7 p.m.

Church services on Sundays would be both in the morning and in the afternoon; the latter service would be at 2 p.m., thus finishing in time for dinner. Lunch was not a separate meal around 1 p.m., but in middle and upper class circles, if visiting at any time during the day, wine and cake would be offered to the visitors.

Travel outside Inverness was by coach. The "Defiance" coach left Inverness every morning at 6 a.m. for Aberdeen; with the return coach arriving in Inverness at 6.30 p.m. The "Star" coach went eastwards via Campbelltown (Ardersier). There was also a mail coach to Edinburgh via the Perth road, leaving Inverness at 6.45 a.m., and the return coach arrived at 6 a.m. Mail coaches also ran to and from Aberdeen and Thurso.

Robert Preece
April 2013

The interior of the 'new' St. John's Chapel from a photograph in the Joseph Cook collection, probably dating from around 1900.

Editorial comment from the 1922 edition:

An interesting document shedding some light on the ecclesiastical history of Inverness during the early part of the 19th century has recently been brought to our notice by Mr Hugh Mackenzie, Tain Cottage, Fairfield Road. It consists of a diary written by the Very Rev. Charles Fyvie, A.M. *[Master of Arts, as then abbreviated],* Dean of Moray and Ross *[possibly also Argyle, or only Moray – sources vary],* who ministered to the Episcopal congregation of Inverness for about thirty years in the first half of last *[19th]* century. The diary came into Mr Mackenzie's possession some years ago, and we gladly avail ourselves of the privilege of submitting some extracts for the information of our readers, prefacing them with some general notes.

During the ecclesiastical troubles of the 17th century these northern parts were much divided. After the Revolution of 1688 Inverness remained much attached to Episcopacy, and a considerable congregation preserved its entity.

When Dr Samuel Johnson paid his memorable visit to the Highlands in 1773, on his way to the Hebrides, he stayed at Inverness, where he attended worship in the "English chapel". Boswell records that this building was "but mean. The altar was a bare fir table, with a coarse stool for kneeling on, covered with a piece of sailcloth doubled by way of cushion." The officiating clergyman (Mr Tait) "read prayers very well, though with much of the Scotch accent."

This Mr Tait, it would appear, was clergyman at Fort-George, and frequently officiated on Sunday afternoon at Inverness "for a guinea, and no less." The resident clergyman at Inverness *[a few years later]*, the Rev. M. *[wrong – should be Andrew]* Macfarlane, was afterwards for many years the well-known Bishop of Ross, Moray, Argyll and the Isles. He was consecrated coadjutor to Bishop *[Arthur]* Petrie at Peterhead in 1787, having been ordained Deacon for Forgue *[near Huntly]* in 1769.

In connection with Dr Johnson's visit to Inverness, it is recorded that Bishop Macfarlane "exhibited his church and organ"– the latter a rare acquisition even in Episcopal circles in Scotland in these days – to the great lexicographer, but it is not recorded whether the worthy Samuel was treated to an exhibition of the musical capacity of what must have been an unpretentious instrument, or what reflections he made by way of indicating his qualifications to pose as a musical critic.[4]

The modest edifice visited by Dr Johnson did duty until 1801, when a small, neat chapel, surmounted by a cupola, was erected near the foot of Church Street, opposite the Gaelic Church *[now Leakey's bookshop]*, as the Episcopal place of worship. This building, which cost £1000, and provided accommodation for 300 sitters, was taken down after the new chapel ("Old St. John's") was opened, and dwelling houses were erected on the site.

Bishop Macfarlane died at Inverness on 26th July 1819, aged 75 years, and was buried in the Chapel-Yard there *[see page 114]*. He was succeeded in the incumbency by the Rev. Charles Fyvie, A.M., who was for thirty years the faithful minister of the congregation. Mr Fyvie was ordained by Bishop *[Alexander]* Jolly at the early age of 20, and shortly afterwards entered on his labours at Inverness, where he became a highly respected and useful citizen. He took a special interest in the poor and needy, was unvarying in his courtesy and hospitality, while his gentleness and benevolence made him beloved by all classes. His sincere attachment to the Episcopal Church of Scotland, and his ceaseless zeal to promote the welfare of the Inverness congregation, had excellent results, and he was

Bishop Alexander Jolly (1798–1838) from a book illustration.

not long settled there when the need of a new church became apparent. With characteristic courage Dean Fyvie faced the situation, and ultimately arrangements were made for the

[4] This information must be an error, as Macfarlane did not start his incumbency in Inverness until 1779; nor is this fact mentioned in Johnson's *Journey to the Western Isles of Scotland*. However, an organ is mentioned in that book as being in the Chapel in Aberdeen, played by a Mr Tait – presumably not the same person who read the Inverness service and was the clergyman for Fort George. Bertie *(see bibliography)* says that St. John's Church was served at this time from Arpafeelie in the Black Isle.

erection of St. John's in Church Street. The foundation stone was laid on 31st March 1837 by Dean Fyvie in presence of the Provost and Magistrates, and the church was finished and opened in *[September]* 1839.

The building was considered handsome, and looked upon as a choice addition to the architectural features of the town. The cost was about £2000. The worthy Dean resided at Roseheath (Hilton House), where he died on 13th February 1849 in the 53rd year of his age. He was a man of the most genial, kindly character, and in all circumstances he was ever the dignified, courtly gentleman. His services were at the command of all classes, and he administered the sacrament of baptism or marriage with equal readiness to nobleman and tinker. The Dean was twice married; his first wife, Miss Janet Adam, died in 1828, in the 32nd year of her age, and his second wife, Miss Duff Macfarlane, a daughter of Bishop Macfarlane, was as noted a personality as her husband.[5]

Bishop Andrew Macfarlane (1787–1798) in a silhouette portrait.

Dean Fyvie's diary begins in 1829 as a Sunday record of events, but after a few months this was discontinued, and a daily diary commenced in 1839, and continued until the close of 1841. The first 26 pages of the manuscript, which are missing, would probably have started at the beginning of 1829. As it is, the first available entry is dated March 22nd. We now proceed to make the following extracts:–

---

[5] For full biographical details about the Fyvie family see pages 115 and 116.

[The diary text in this edition is in full, and not just extracts as was the case in the 1922 edition.]

1829

March 22 (3 Lent) – Had notice during the week of the death of Mr *[Hugh]* Buchan at Elgin *[Dean of the Diocese from 1787]*, and resolved to go there to attend his funeral. Preached in the morning from Luke xix.10 – "The Son of Man is come to seek and to save that which was lost." I introduced into this sermon some remarks on the general neglect of the Lent season, and the bad attendance at week-day prayers; whether well or ill received, I was resolved to do my duty in this respect, for I am convinced that if members of the Episcopal Church once lose sight of their distinctive principles, that Church cannot long maintain its ground. In the afternoon preached from St. John viii.11 *["Go and sin no more"]*; this sermon was chiefly compiled from one of Bishop Jebb's *[John Jebb, Bishop of Limerick, 1822–1834]*.

March 29 (4 Lent) – Went, as I proposed, to Elgin on Monday, accompanied by Mr *[Duncan]* Mackenzie *[incumbent, Strathnairn, 1817–1858, affectionally known as 'Parson Duncan']*. Mr Buchan's interment took place on Tuesday. I was called upon to read part of the burial service at the grave, which I did, Mr *[Alexander]* Shand *[Dean of Aberdeen]* joining with me. I had the satisfaction, upon this occasion, of meeting my friend Mr Bruce. Spent a day also with Sir A. D.'s family *[Sir Archibald Dunbar, 6th Bart, of Northfield, Duffus House, 1772–1849 – Fyvie had been the family tutor]*, which is always a pleasure. Mr Buchan *(Rev. Hugh Buchan, incumbent, Elgin)* died much respected by all classes. He died on Wednesday, the 18th, in the 71st year of his age. Preached twice, as usual, this Sunday, but with difficulty, having a severe headache.

April 5 (5 Lent) – Preached this forenoon from Isaiah v.3-4 *["Judge betwixt me and my vineyard"]* – the discourses compiled chiefly from Bp. *[Charles]* Summer's *[Bishop of Llandaff, 1826, Bishop of Winchester 1827–1869]* on the same text. I altered the style slightly. The discourse was most decidedly a favourite and was <u>most attentively</u> listened to, but the audience was not numerous, the day being very cold. In the afternoon preached from 1John iii.2-3 *["... it doth not yet appear what we shall be, but we know that, when he doth appear, we shall be like him; for we shall see him as he is"]*, a sermon formerly delivered. Dined afterwards with a friend in town, and returned home in the evening. Had a letter from Dr *[Michael]* Russel *[incumbent at Leith, later Dean of Edinburgh]* this morning, inviting me to take up my abode with him while attending the Synod in Edinburgh next June.

April 12 (S. before Easter) – Felt very unfit for the duties of this day, and preached in the forenoon only on the Atonement from Isaiah liii.2-3. The weather being still very unfavourable the congregation was not numerous. I announced the public services for the week and read the exhortation to the communion preparatory to the Festival of Easter.

April 17 (Good Friday) – The congregation was more numerous than I expected. I preached from 1Cor. i.18 *[The preaching of the Cross is to them who perish foolishness ...]*, partly original and partly altered from Le Bas *[Charles Webbe Le Bas, Fellow of Trinity College, Cambridge]* "Discourses on Christ Crucified". The sermon was listened to with great attention, and seemed to make an impression. In the evening I rode out to Dores to baptise a child, and returned home late.

April 19 (Easter) – Read prayers, and preached a sermon on the H*[oly]* Sacrament on Easter Eve. After coming out of church Mr Wilson *[possibly William Scot Wilson, incumbent at Fortrose, 1827–1832]* joined me. As I had the necessary arrangements to make for the administration of the Sacrament we remained in town till the evening. Everything seemed favourable for the services of this happy day; the morning was very fine, and corresponded well with the bright hopes and glorious prospects emanating from our Lord's Resurrection. Mr Wilson read the morning service, and I preached from Romans viii, 34: "Who is he that condemneth? It is Christ who died, etc." There were 82 communicants, a greater number than on any former occasion.

April 26 (1 S. after Easter) – Explained the doctrine of absolution as understood in the Protestant Episcopal Churches in a discourse from John xx.22-23, delivered in the forenoon; in the afternoon preached on the certainty of human resurrection from 1Thes. iv.14.

May 3 (2 S. after Easter) – Preached in the morning from John xv.4-5 "As the branch cannot abide in the vine, etc." The congregation was not numerous, which I regretted the more especially as this discourse appeared to attract very particular attention from those who were present. It was chiefly original with some altered quotations from Stanhope *[George Stanhope, Dean of Canterbury, 1739 and later editions]*, and a passage towards the close altered from Bishop *[John]* Sumners' sermon on the same text *[Bishop of Chester, later Archbishop of Canterbury]*. This sermon may with propriety be preached again soon. Preached in the afternoon on keeping holy the Sabbath from Isaiah lviii.13-14. The arrangement of this discourse is taken from Bishop Jebb's on the same text.

May 10 (3 Easter) – Preached in the forenoon from Romans viii.14 on spiritual influences, pointing out the distinction between the extraordinary operation of the Holy Spirit (in the early times of the Gospel) for special purposes, and the operation of grace which are always necessary for the sanctification of Christians of every age. In the afternoon preached on the subject of temptation from 2Pet. ii.9.

May 17 (4 Easter) – Preached in the forenoon on the Redeemer's gracious invitation to sinners, "Come unto me all ye that travail and are heavy laden and I will give you rest"; and in the afternoon from 1John iv.18, a sermon formerly preached, and which was originally compiled from two sermons of Le Bas upon the same subject, viz. on the fear of God and the love of God, when the Christian may be said to be actuated by the former as a motive to obedience, and when by the latter.

May 24 (5 Easter) – Followed up the subject of my sermon last Sunday forenoon, in a discourse on Matthew xi.28-29, on the easiness of Christ's yolk, introducing some quotations from a sermon of Bp. Sumner's, and from one by Archdeacon Pott *[Archdeacon of St. Albans, 1789–1812]* on the same text. In the afternoon preached on Prayer from St. John xvi.23-24. On the Thursday previous officiated in the Garrison Chapel at Fort-George, and administered the Holy Communion, and preached my Sermon on the "Vine and the branches" which I had delivered at Inverness on the 2nd Sunday after Easter. Dined afterwards with Captain Tapp, and returned home in the evening in company with Miss Macfarlane *(who afterwards became the Dean's second wife)*, whom I met at Campbelltown *[Ardersier]* on her way to Inverness from Elgin.

May 31 (S. after Ascension) – Preached in the forenoon on the influences of God's Holy Spirit in the hearts of believers, and in the afternoon on Christ's intercession at the right hand of God; both discourses appropriate to the season and preparatory to Whitsunday, and both preached on a similar occasion before. On Ascension Day I read prayers and preached as usual, but much cause to complain of bad attendance, the number present being very small although the day was very fine.

June 7 (Whitsunday) – This day there were sixty communicants and the service very numerously attended. Mr Wilson read prayers in the morning and assisted at the altar. I preached a sermon proper for the festival from John xiv.15-16, and Mr Wilson read the service in the evening, while I went to administer the sacrament to some sick people.

June 14 (Trinity S.) – Preached in the forenoon a discourse on Prayer composed two years ago (Col. iv.2); some of the leading ideas were taken from one of the chapters in Law's "Christian Perfection" *[William Law, 1720's]*, in which he treats of the subject of prayer. I consider this discourse a very useful one, and it was listened to with much attention. In the afternoon preached from Luke xi.28 *["Blessed are they that hear the word of God, and keep it"]*. In this discourse are some passages taken from a sermon of Bp. Jebb's on the same subject.

June 21 (1 Trinity) – I spent this Sunday in Edinburgh whither I had gone as delegate from the Diocese to attend a General Synod summoned for the 24th. Attended St. John's Chapel in the morning, and heard Bp. Sandford *[Bishop of Edinburgh]* preach; in the afternoon heard Mr Sinclair at St. Paul's. I left Inverness by the mail on Monday evening (the 15th), and arrived at Banff the next morning and after spending two days with my esteemed friends Mr and Mrs Bruce, there, they accompanied me on Thursday morning to Keith; here I joined Miss Macfarlane, who proceeded with me to Edinburgh, next day, from Aberdeen. In my absence Mr Wilson officiated at Inverness, and the Miss Mackintoshes kindly undertook to stay at Culcabock and take care of my children till my return. While at Banff I had accounts of a fatal accident that occurred near Elgin on Monday the 15th, James Fraser, youngest son of Mr Fraser, Ness-side, having been drowned while bathing in the Lossie, and his tutor on attempting to rescue him, unfortunately came by the same fate. The little boy Fraser lived for some years in my house, and was a very promising, kind-hearted creature.

June 28 (2 Trinity) – After attending the Synod on Wednesday, I remained in Edinburgh till Friday evening. I travelled by the mail to Perth where I overtook Bp. Low on his way to Inverness for the purpose of holding his triennial visitation. We started in company on Saturday morning by the Highland road and arrived safely at Inverness at 9 o'clock. The following day having been previously fixed for Mr Wilson's ordination in my Chapel, I preached the ordination sermon from Gal. vi.9-10 – "Be not weary in well doing". Mr Mackenzie and Mr P*[aul]* Maccol *[incumbent, Appin, 1810—1838]* were present and assisted at the ordination, and afterwards 50 of the congregation received the Holy Communion along with the Bishop and Clergy. In the afternoon I read the service, and Bp. Low preached. The Rev. W. Fraser, formerly Chaplain at Banares *[Benares, now Varanasi, India]*, attended Church forenoon and afternoon, but took no part in the service. The Bishop, Mr Mackenzie, Mr Maccol and Mr Wilson dined and spent the remainder of the day at my house; this day was upon the whole quite satisfactory, the Chapel was full, and the service impressive, and the number of communicants much greater than I had anticipated, so soon after Whitsunday.

July 5 (3 Trinity) – The Rev. Wm. Fraser preached forenoon and afternoon, and spent the remainder of the day with me. We had a great deal of religious conversation, greatly to my satisfaction. A day spent in company with such a man as Mr Fraser is a bright spot to look back upon. On Wednesday the 1st, Bp. Low delivered a charge to the Clergy in my Chapel, and Mr Wilson preached the visitation sermon from "We do all things, dearly beloved, for your edifying" *[2Cor. xii.19]*. The Bp. afterwards confirmed nine young members of my congregation, most of whom were above eighteen years of age, The Bp. and all the clergy dined together in the afternoon at the Caledonian Hotel, as it is the practice on such occasions for the Bp. to entertain his clergy. We spent the evening most agreeably, had a good deal of promiscuous conversation on the state of the Church, and next morning the Bp. set out for Ross-shire.

July 12 (4 Trinity) – Several incidents of a distressing nature occurred during this week. On the evening of Sunday the 5th, a child of Mr Alexr. Mackintosh's, London, died very suddenly at Daviot House; and on Wednesday, while I was proceeding with the burial service at the child's funeral, I received an express from Mr R. Grant requesting my immediate presence at Cantray, as Lady Davidson was considered in a state of immediate danger. I set off immediately in company with Dr Robertson, but before we arrived Lady Davidson was in a state of stupor, which rendered both the physician's presence and mine of no avail, and early the following morning she expired, being the very day fixed for the marriage of her daughter to Mr Grant. I returned home in the evening, but too late to see Bp. Low, who set out next morning for Argyleshire. On Friday Mr Fraser called, and as I said I wished to go to Cantray on Saturday he very kindly offered to preach for me on Sunday forenoon (this day). He did so accordingly. In the afternoon Mr Fraser read prayers and I preached from 1Cor. xiii.12. *["For now we see in a mirror, dimly, but then face to face. Now I know in part, but then I shall know just as I also am known."]*

(Mr Grant above referred to was Sir Robert Grant, son of Mr Charles Grant, M.P. for Inverness-shire from 1802 till 1818, a noted Indian statesman, for a time the Chairman of the Board of Directors of the East India Company, and brother of Mr Charles Grant, Lord Glenelg, who entered Parliament in 1811 as representative of the Inverness Burghs, serving in that capacity until 1818, when he succeeded his father as member for Inverness County, and continued to represent the constituency until his elevation to the Peerage as Lord Glenelg in 1835. Sir Robert Grant was elected member of Parliament for the Elgin Burghs in 1818, and for the Inverness Burghs in 1826, representing this constituency for four years. In 1830 and 1831 he was returned for Norwich, and in 1832 for Finsbury. Sir Robert was

appointed Judge Advocate-General, and in 1834 was appointed Governor of Bombay, receiving the honour of knighthood. Sir Robert Grant, whose marriage to Margaret, only daughter of Sir David Davidson of Cantray, took place on 11th August 1829, died in India in 1838. There was a family of two sons and two daughters, namely, Sir Charles Grant, K.C.S.I., formerly a member of Council of India; Colonel Robert Grant, R.E., Deputy Adjutant-General; Sibyll Sophia, married to Mr Granville Ryder, a nephew of Dudley, 2nd Earl of Harrowby; and Constance Charemile, who died in childhood. Sir David Davidson of Cantray, born 20th July 1788, married in December 1804 Margaret Rose of the family of Kilravock. Sir David was knighted in 1812, and died at the early age of 30, on 28th March 1818.)

July 19 (5 Trinity) – Preached in the forenoon from Rom. v.19: "As by one man's disobedience, etc."; and in the afternoon from Ps.119.96: "I have seen an end of all perfection, etc." Nothing particular occurred this week, except that on Monday the 13th I attended Lady Davidson's funeral and performed the burial service at the family Burying Ground, in the Churchyard of Croy.

July 26 (6 Trinity) – The Chapel was unusually full today. I preached in the forenoon from 2Cor. xiii.14. "The grace of our Lord Jesus Christ, and the love of God, and the fellowship of the Holy Ghost, be with you all." The composition of this sermon occupied me for nearly ten days, as it embraced a great deal of doctrinal and practical illustration; it was very attentively heard, and seemed suitable for a mixed audience. In the afternoon preached 2Tim. iii.16-17: on the inspiration of the Scriptures.

August 2 (7 Trinity) – I preached the forenoon on the opposition manifested by mankind against the doctrines of the Gospel. The sermon was preached before, with a different text. In the afternoon preached from "The Son of Man is come to seek and save that which was lost." (Luke xix.10) There were some extracts in this sermon from one of Bp. Sumner's on the same text. There was a considerable number of strangers present, and amongst others the Earl of Harrowby [Dudley Ryder, 2nd Baron Harrowby, 1762–1847] and one of his sons.

August 9 (8 Trinity) – This week again has been marked by a very afflicting occurrence, the sudden death of the only surviving child of Mr Alexr. Mackintosh, who only three weeks ago lost a child at Daviot, as already mentioned on the last page. Mrs Mackintosh requested me to preach this day from Rev. xiv.13: "Blessed are the dead which die in the Lord, etc." Under circumstances so peculiarly distressing, I readily complied with her request, as she wished to be present herself. The composition was too hastily put together, but as my feelings were much engaged on the subject, I addressed myself chiefly to the heart and the effect was greater than I expected. In the afternoon I read prayers but being much fatigued I did not preach.

August 16 (9 Trinity) – This Sunday the Holy Sacrament was administered. There were 50 communicants. I preached in the forenoon on universal redemption from 1Tim. iii.10, "The living God who is the Saviour of all men, and especially of those that believe." In the afternoon from 1Cor. xi.29: "He that eateth and drinketh unworthily eateth and drinketh damnation to himself, etc."; explained the meaning of this text, by reference to the local circumstances and practices to which St. Paul alludes in the exhortation to the Corinthians concerning the irregularities committed at the celebration of the Lord's Supper – pointed out how far this language is applicable as a warning to Christians of the present day, etc. After evening service administered the sacrament to Mr Fraser, Ness-side.

August 23 (10 Trinity) – Nothing occurred this day or during the week that is worth noting. I preached in the forenoon from Rom. v.1 on Justification. In the evening from 1Tim. v.22 on being partakers of other men's sins.

August 30 (11 Trinity) – The foregoing attempt at a Sunday Diary was discontinued from this date.

C. F.

[Below this entry are some other entries: the first one is a faint copy of the August 30 entry. The second entry is difficult to read and in a different hand . Both might be by a child copying the text as a writing exercise. Similar entries appear elsewhere in the text, and have not been transcribed here.]

Editorial comment from the 1922 edition:

On the page opposite the last of the Sunday entries the diary is resumed as a daily record beginning with the year 1839. It is greatly to be regretted that the worthy Dean's observations of the ten intervening years are not recorded. To the congregation of St. John's these years were of special importance, and numerous interesting events took place. In particular there was the beginning of the new church, the foundation stone of which was laid on Thursday 31st August 1837. Despite the fact that the weather was very unfavourable the ceremony was performed with order and solemnity. There were no masonic procession or masonic honours introduced, the ceremony used being wholly of a religious character. Dean Fyvie purposely avoided a more public display, judging the service compiled by himself was more suitable for the occasion. After a suitable address and prayer by Mr Fyvie (he was not yet Dean) the foundation stone was adjusted, and a bottle deposited in it containing an Inverness newspaper of the day; and an inscription with the names of the Bishop of the Diocese, and the gentlemen of the committee of management. Mr Fyvie laid the mallet on the foundation stone three times, repeating the words "In the name of God the Father, God the Son, and God the Holy Ghost." After the reading of several Scripture lessons the Rev. Mr *[William]* Oldfield *[Curate, Pittenweem, Fife, but at this point ministering in Skye and the Uists]* concluded the proceedings with a fervent prayer, the whole of which is preserved in the "Inverness Courier".

To Invernessians of that time the building of St. John's Church was an object of special interest, and in the early part of 1838, as the sacred building progressed, its elegance attracted attention, and a good idea of the style and workmanship of the edifice when completed could be formed. When the doorway was finished it was pronounced as uncommonly rich and massive.

An outstanding event in connection with St. John's congregation took place on Friday, 27th July 1838, when the Right Rev. Bishop Low held a public ordination in the Old Chapel at which Mr Alexander Ewing, described as "of the College", Elgin, was admitted to the sacred Order of Deacons *[for the Diocese of Ross and Argyll, later Bishop of Argyll and the Isles]*. Prayers were read by the Rev. W. J. Copland of

Trinity College, Oxford, while the sermon was preached by Mr Fyvie on the individual responsibility of the Christian minister, the solemn proceedings being concluded with the celebration of Holy Communion. Such a ceremony had not taken place in Inverness for many years, the greater part of the congregation had probably never witnessed such a ceremony before.

On the following Sunday the Bishop closed his triennial visitation with a confirmation at Dingwall. During the visitation he confirmed in all 142 members made up as follows:– Isle of Skye, 11; Appin, 47; Fort William, 11; Strathnairn, 11; Inverness, 26; Arpafeelie, 19; Dingwall and Highfield, 17.

The Rev. David Low, of Pittenweem *[Fife]*, was chosen Bishop of Ross in 1819. He had visited the Highlands twice before his consecration, in the years 1805 and 1810, and thus was familiar with the duties which he had to perform. To Bishop Low the Episcopal Church in the Highlands owes a deep debt of gratitude. He was assiduous in his visitations, founded new congregations, and infused new life into others. He died *[on]* 26th January 1855 in the 88th year of his age.

The Right Rev. David Low, Bishop of Moray, 1838–1850.

In the portion of Dean Fyvie's diary already given, no reference is made to the weather, neither does he make any allusion to church music. In the following portions of the diary, however, allusions to both of these subjects are frequent and pointed; in the matter of congregational music it is, indeed, quite apparent that the Dean was an enthusiast. We now resume extracts from the diary:–

[Again, in this edition the text is reproduced in full, and is not simply extracts]

1839

January 1: Weather very rough and stormy, very few attended Church. In the evening dined at Dr Munro's *[Viewmount, Culduthel Road]*.

January 2: Attended Mr Sheppard's funeral *(Mr Alex. Sheppard, Town Clerk [and local solicitor])*; afterwards baptised the Methodist Minister's child at Millburn on my way home; baptised another child (of a Mr Baker's) who expired before the service was concluded – the scene altogether very singular.

January 3: The weather uncommonly boisterous; Dr and Mrs Munro dined and passed the evening at Roseheath, talked with him about Oxford Tracts, Froude's "Remains", etc. *[Richard Froude was an Anglican priest and an early leader of the Oxford Movement, died 1836; Froude's "Remains" were edited by John Henry Newman and John Keble, and published in two volumes in 1838–1839.]*

January 4: Snow fairly set in with high wind; attended the funeral of the infant who died two days before while I was in the act of baptising it.

January 5: Practising of sacred music in the Chapel with the choir, and pleased with their improvement; towards evening a deal of snow fell, and for some hours drifted very much.

January 6: Sunday and the Feast of the Epiphany. Weather still stormy and Chapel thinly attended in consequence. Made annual collection for the N. Infirmary *[later the Royal Northern Infirmary, established in the 1790's but opened in 1803]* (£13.10/-); received a note from Raigmore in the morning with an order for Fifty Pounds to be immediately applied for the benefit of the poor. Mr Mackenzie and Lady Anne Mackenzie of Scatwell were in Church, both services, and contributed five pounds to the collection for the Infirmary. *(Mr Mackenzie, who succeeded his father in the estates and the baronetcy in 1843 as Sir James John Randell Mackenzie, married 10th October 1838 [to] Lady Anne Wentworth Fitzwilliam, daughter of the 5th Earl Fitzwilliam.)*

January 7: Monday. In the morning received a note from Raigmore enclosing an order for 100 barrels of coals for the poor of Inverness, in addition to the £50 sent yesterday; was busy all day in getting coals and meal distributed by ticket through the District Visiting Society. Weather exceedingly stormy, and thermometer unprecedentedly low in the morning.

January 8: Snow falling all day and drifts in the evening; dined at

Raigmore's and met Mr J. and Lady Anne Mackenzie.

January 9: Snow very deep, but sky clear and weather pleasant for the season; attended practising of choir, and walked afterwards into the country with Dr Munro.

January 10: Day, rain and sleet throughout, did some business in town in the forenoon, and in the evening finished reading the 2nd volume of Prideax's [sic] "Connection" [Humphrey Prideaux: "The Old and New Testament connected, in the History of the Jews and Neighbouring Nations ... to the Time of Christ", published 1716–1718]: a highly valuable book written in a very pleasing style (the third time I have read it through).

January 11: Weather clear and a thorough thaw, snow mainly cleared away from the low grounds. In the forenoon occupied in procuring a supply of meal for the poor, there being none in town. In the evening partly occupied as usual in teaching the children, and partly in making preparation for Sunday.

January 12: Occupied much the same as yesterday; weather much the same.

January 13: (Sunday): Chapel thinly attended; wind and rain in violent gusts; nothing particular to note as to the service.

January 14: Read in the newspapers most afflicting accounts of loss of life and property at sea on Monday the 7th, at the time the thermometer was so low in Inverness; in the evening took a copy of one of the ribs in the roof of the Cathedral at Cologne as a pattern for those of our new chapel – they are said to be the most perfectly beautiful in the world.

January 15: Nothing particular occurred beyond the usual routine; dined in the evening at Mr G. Anderson's and met Mr Mackenzie of Scatwell and Lady Anne; she talked with great vivacity about the Queen [Victoria], the coronation, etc. I returned home at night in their carriage.

January 16: Clear sky and hard frost, very pleasant; attended practising in the chapel and afterwards walked to Muirtown; in the evening wrote a long letter to Bishop Low.

January 17: Attended Mrs Jameson's funeral and paid several professional visits afterwards; in the evening dined at Dr Munro's with a party. Mrs F. not very well and stayed at home.

January 18: Began to thaw about 2 o'clock and became mild; made several enquiries about poor people in town along with Mrs. F.;

afterwards called at Mrs Fraser's, Ness Cottage *[Haugh Road]*. I found them all at home; talked about <u>Poor Laws</u> and increase of pauperism, etc.

January 19: Nothing occurred worth mentioning; attended practising of sacred music in the Chapel; in the evening finished my sermons for Sunday. Reading *[Joseph]* Bingham's "Ecclesiastical Antiquities" *[first published from 1710]* – a very valuable book: all clergymen ought to study it attentively. Mem.: In the early ages the laity were sometimes called "idiots", Bishops called "God's Beadles".

January 20 (Sunday): Nothing particular in this service; music very good; congregation as usual very attentive; dined in the evening with Dr Munro, and had a great deal of interesting conversation on <u>Primitive Christianity</u>, etc.; returned home at 9 o'clock.

January 21: Made several calls, and had an interview with Raigmore about distribution of poor's money; in the evening read part of the January number of "The British Critic and Quarterly Theological Review", and wrote some letters. Weather cold, but clear and pleasant.

January 22: Finished the no. of the "British Critic"; walked to Muirtown with Mrs F. in the forenoon to bid good-bye to Mrs Warrand's daughter, previously to going to England to school; dined late, and read the whole evening afterwards.

January 23: A beautiful spring-looking day; engaged in business about sale of United Charities' Buildings; attended practising and baptised a child in the Chapel, using one of Mr Bowdler's fonts for the first time. Dined in the evening with Mrs F. at Ness Cottage.

January 24: Weather still very fine, variously occupied during the forenoon, about Charity Buildings again; and about subscriptions for the poor; in the evening as usual teaching the children, etc., reading though Bingham and Prideaux' "Connections".

January 25: St. Paul's Day. Nothing happened worthy of notice; weather uncommonly fine; delivered to Mr Mackintosh the Font and Chalice sent by Mr Bowdler for Strathnairn.

January 26: Wrote a sermon on the <u>Christian Race</u>; original throughout; sat up late; wrote to Capt. Duff; dined for the first time this year by daylight; Col. and Mrs Falconer called in the morning; thought that we ought to pay attention to military men, as having peculiar claims upon us – hazardous life comfort, etc., for very poor remuneration; attended musical practising, and pleased with performance.

January 27 (Sunday): Preached the sermon on the Christian Race composed yesterday; a good congregation and the service altogether very satisfactory; the sermon listened to with great attention.

January 28: Taken ill during the night with violent pains in the back and stomach, and this day have been entirely confined to my room; weather very cold and unpleasant; read a whole volume of Prideaux' "Connections". The amount of crime there recorded is quite appalling.

January 29: Greatly better today (D.G.) *[Dei gratia = by the grace of God]*: went to town to see some sick people; saw in the newspapers that the Queen Dowager *[Adelaide, widow of William IV]* was about to build a church for the Anglican residents at Malta at the expense of £8000. The Church of England has always neglected its outposts and Colonial branches, a sin which seems to have been manifestly visited in return; observed a letter in the "St. James' Chronicle" in reference to the Oxford Memorial that Empire Bishops were not called Prelates until the time of William the Conqueror, called so as Barons. Prelate no ecclesiastical name, but bestowed by Kings, and may be taken away by them; Bishops the proper appellation.

January 30: Heavy storm from the north-east with more drifting than I have ever seen in this neighbourhood; received a very unpleasant letter from Admiral Duff to which I replied immediately in a very few words, and in the evening scrolled *[= drafted]* a reply of greater length to be sent tomorrow.

January 31: Storm still continued, but no drift – finished my letter to Admiral Duff; made several calls in the forenoon, and in the evening finished reading the 4th volume of Prideaux – much struck with the character and fate of Marianne, second and favourite wife of Herod. Herod's character is pure and cruel self throughout, no person who knows his general character can doubt the probability of his ordering the infants at Bethlehem to be slain.

February 1: Storm abated but snow deep, and several mails due; had an excellent letter from Mrs R. Macfarlane about Keble *[John Keble: churchman, poet, leader of Oxford Movement]*, poetry, etc. In hearing the children *[at]* their Latin lessons in the evening a curious idea struck me that the "toga pretexta" of the Romans answered to what we call in more homely language a "pin-before" – it was worn by the Roman youth till they were 17, at which stage they took the "toga viriles".

February 2: Nothing particular occurred worth mentioning; made several professional calls in the forenoon, and in the evening concluded my preparations for Sunday; called at Muirtown for Mrs Warrand, along with Dr Munro.

February 3 (Sunday): This is the 10th anniversary of our marriage day. The church was pretty full. After morning service, while in the vestry, I received a letter from Bishop Low, with an instrument prefixed, appointing me Dean of the United Diocese of Moray, Ross and Argyle.

February 4: Nothing occurred worth noting – weather mild.

February 5: do.   do.   do.

February 6: do.   do.   do.

February 7: Fast before the Sacrament in the Kirk *(The Dean always refers to the Church of Scotland as the Kirk)*; wrote several letters and finished reading a vol. of Bingham; walked out with Mrs. F. through the fields; air quite soft and balmy.

February 8: Wrote several letters; made arrangements for distributing meal and coals among the poor people in the town; weather continues mild; generally squally through the night.

February 9: Attended practising, made professional calls; in the evening made arrangements for Sunday. Observed in Bingham's "Ecclesiastical Antiquities" that the name of <u>pagans</u> was given to the <u>heathens</u> after the introduction of Christianity because the greatest relicks *[sic]* of them were in the <u>country villages</u> (pagi), the inhabitants of the large towns having been sooner converted to the faith of Christ's, pagans meaning <u>persons living in villages</u>; this reminds one again of Bishops in the Primitive Church having been called "<u>God's Beadles</u>", and the lay persons having been called idiotai, "<u>idiots</u>". In Wickliffe's translation of the New Testament the word "<u>gelding</u>" is used for "<u>eunuch</u>"; and the word "<u>knave</u>" for servant.

February 10 (Sunday): Chapel tolerably full, and service satisfactory, music in the afternoon admirable, in the morning a little defective; voluntary in the afternoon on 4 b^s *[meaning not established, but could be musically "four flats", or a repeated note]* beautiful. Dr Munro came to tea in the evening; we talked as usual on various religious subjects.

February 11: Occupied most of the day in writing letters, and taking copies; received an excellent letter from Mr Walker of Huntly; finished the second volume of Bingham – a most valuable volume;

ought to be recommended to all young clergymen, and students in theology.

February 12: Nothing occurred worthy of notice; made some calls in the forenoon; in the evening dined at Dr Munro's; met Mr Burke; had some interesting conversations about Scotland's system of theological study. Mr B.'s remarks clear and forcible.

February 13 (Ash Wednesday): Service in Chapel in the forenoon; read the Commination Office *[a service denouncing God's anger and judgements against sinners]* all through – no sermon. In the evening had a letter from James Loch, Esq., M.P. *[Estate Commissioner for the Duke of Sutherland, and M.P. for the Wick Burghs 1832–1852]*, requesting me to read the Burial Service at the interment of the Duchess-Countess of Sutherland in the Cathedral of Dornoch on Wednesday the 20th – claim of precedence by Rev. Mr Kennedy *(Parish Minister of Dornoch)* very amusing.

[Elizabeth Sutherland Leveson-Gower, née Gordon, 1765–1839, 19th Countess of Sutherland. She succeeded to her father's titles in 1766, a few weeks after her first birthday. In September 1785 she married Lord George Leveson-Gower, 1758–1833. The Countess died in London, and her remains were taken by steamer to Aberdeen and thence by land to Dunrobin. The coffin then lay in state in the Castle for three days.]

February 14: Went to town in the forenoon to meet the funeral procession of the Duchess on the way to Dunrobin Castle; called at Mrs Fraser's, Ness Cottage, on my way home. The river <u>uncommonly high</u> – during the previous night it blew from the south-west <u>a perfect hurricane</u>.

February 15: Nothing occurred worthy of notice; weather very stormy; dined at Mr A. Robertson's, Altnaskiach Cottage *[off Culduthel Road]*.

February 16: Weather state very stormy; dined at Baillie Cumming's to meet Grieshernish *[a Laird from the Isle of Skye]*; came home early.

February 17 (Sunday): Deep snow and a good deal of drift. The church very thin; singing very good; preached twice as usual.

February 18: Very busily occupied all day in various duties, and in preparation for my journey to Dunrobin Castle; dined in the evening at Mr G. Anderson's and met the Roman Catholic gentlemen Mr Ch———m, and Mr McD., Glenalladale; the latter repeated a saying of an Irish Roman Catholic, with great good humour. "Blest be the

Council of Trent; they forbad us to eat, but they did not forbid us to drink", – alluding to the Lent fast.

February 19: Slept on the previous night at the Caledonian Hotel and started this morning at 6 in a coach and four horses for Dunrobin Castle, along with Mr Macneil of Colonsay, Mr Macdonald, Lochinver, and Mr Lewis, factor on the Duke of Sutherland's English estates. Had a very pleasant journey, and arrived at Golspie at 11 p.m. after dining and changing horses at Bonar Bridge; weather very cold with a good deal of snow.

February 20: Passed the day at Dunrobin Castle, being the day previous to the Duchess's funeral; met the Hon. Mr Howard, Lord Edward Howard *[both related to the Earls of Carlisle]*, Hon. F. Egerton *[second son of the Duchess, 1st Earl of Ellesmere]*, Mr Loch, M.P., Mr W. Mackenzie, W.S., Rev. Mr Kennedy, etc. Slept in the Castle; splendid mansion, romantically situated, and the whole establishment very princely.

February 21: The funeral procession left the Castle at a quarter past 10, consisting of a great number of carriages and gentlemen on horseback. The hearse was drawn by six horses, preceded by 12 gentlemen on horseback and 4 mutes mounted; a vast concourse of tenantry joined the procession as it advanced, especially at the Mound, where about 3000 were assembled, or rather stationed, for they merely stood uncovered while the procession passed. I read the burial service in the Cathedral of Dornoch, where the body was deposited in a vault below the chancel. This ancient cathedral is now beautifully restored to nearly its original splendour, and is really very handsome *[paid for mainly by the Duchess between 1835 and 1837]*. The solemnity was altogether very striking and solemn, and strongly impressed my mind with deeply serious thoughts. Returned in the evening along with Mr Lewis and Mr Mackenzie, W.S., as far as Bonar Bridge, where we remained all night. Weather excessively cold and stormy.

February 22: Started at 6 o'clock from Bonar Bridge and arrived safely at Inverness about 7 in the evening.

February 23: Made preparation for Sunday; attended practising, etc.; felt very unwell in the afternoon and continued so most of the night.

February 24 (Sunday): Contrary to expectations was able (thank God) to perform two full services as usual, the Chapel pretty full, and the music remarkably good. On Saturday I had administered the Holy Sacrament to Miss Catharine Bethune at Dr Munro's, and he came into the Vestry after Morning service to tell me that she had expired about nine in the evening. The past has been on the whole rather an exciting week, but as these pages are only intended as a brief record of <u>occurrences</u>, reflections are purposely omitted as unsuitable to my object in making these notes.

February 25: Variously occupied in the forenoon; in the evening wrote circular letters to the clergy of the United Diocese of Moray, Ross and Argyle, with queries to be answered respecting their livings, for the purpose of transmission to the Secretary of the Scottish Episcopal Church Society.

February 26: Walked to Muirtown in the forenoon, the weather mild, but with a good deal of wind, nothing occurred worthy of notice.

February 27: Read the burial office at the interment of Miss Catharine Bethune; in the evening dined at Dr Munro's with Rev. Mr Bethune of Dingwall.

February 28: Occupied in the forenoon in business; attended a meeting about the poor; unpleasant business about Infant School; in the evening read Oxford Tracts and wrote several letters.

March 1: Weather very mild, with wind from the south; in the forenoon attended several meetings, about Savings Bank, etc. etc.; in the evening occupied as usual in reading; also wrote some letters.

March 2: Wrote a sermon for Sunday from Phil. ii.12-13 *["Work out your own salvation with fear and trembling"]*; attended practising in the forenoon; engaged in the evening in finishing my sermon and in making other preparations for Sunday.

March 3 (Sunday, 3 Lent): Chapel unusually full for the season of the year, both forenoon and afternoon; sermon listened to with great attention and I hope with profit. Music excellent throughout, great improvement in the singing. After service received a letter from Rev. Mr Drummond, announcing a proposed visit of Rev. Mr Hodgson at Inverness on behalf of the Church Missionary Society.

March 4: Nothing particular occurred worthy of notice; weather fine.

March 5: Made professional visits in the forenoon; dined at Mr Peter Anderson's; evening remarkably beautiful, and the appearance of the heavens exceedingly striking.

March 6: Rev. Mr Hodgson read prayers in the Chapel; heard of the sudden death of Thomas Mackenzie Paterson, on whom I had called the previous day (he being then in perfect good health); went to see his orphan children. In the evening dined at Raigmore's along with Mr Hodgson, and made arrangements to accompany him to

Dingwall on the following day.

March 7: Accompanied Mr Hodgson to Dingwall as proposed; had a meeting on behalf of the Church of England Missionary Society in the Parish Church which was numerously attended; a collection was made which amounted to £10; dined afterwards at Rev. Mr Bethune's, and returned home in the evening by Kessock ferry; weather <u>excessively</u> cold with easterly wind and a little snow. Mr Hodgson's account of the Missions was very interesting and delivered with more simplicity than generally accompanies such narrations. Mr Macdonald of Ferintosh *(Rev. Dr Macdonald, parish and Free Church minister of Urquhart from 1812 to 1849, popularly known throughout the Highlands as the Apostle of the North)* attended the meeting and dined with us at Mr Bethune's, and told some very good anecdotes – one of a lady who was in search of a pure church as nothing less would suit her views; she was told (I think by Mr Newton): "Madam, if you find this pure church, and you become a member of it, it will no longer be a pure church"; this is said to have convinced the lady of the extravagance of her views.

March 8: Had a meeting in the Chapel on behalf of the Church Missionary Society; I opened the proceedings with prayer and Mr Hodgson delivered a very interesting address, with intelligence, calmness and good Christian feeling, with no fanaticism or extravagance of any kind. Day very cold with hard frost and some snow. Mr Hodgson told me of a clergyman who denominated his own preaching as "spiritual champagne" which he seemed to think a very acceptable beverage. I fear there is too much of such champagne dealt out, where plain wholesome fare would be more useful and necessary.

March 9: Read the burial office at the interment of Mr Paterson; afterwards attended practising in the Chapel, and made preparations for the Sunday. Weather still excessively cold with intense frost.

March 10 (Sunday): Church tolerably full; preached two sermons on self-denial which were considered good; the music was excellent. After evening service heard that Mrs Sherriff was thought to be in a dying state.

March 11: Nothing occurred worthy of note.

March 12: Heard of the death of Mrs Sherriff; passed the evening at Dr Munro's, with a few gentlemen, previously to his leaving for the West Indies.

March 13: Prayers in Chapel, and afterwards attended a meeting at the Northern Infirmary. Weather fine; dined again at Dr Munro's with

Mrs Fyvie.

March 14: Wrote several letters in the morning; went to Moniack *[a short distance west of Inverness]* to visit Mrs Sherriff's family in their affliction; returned home to dinner, and went at 10 to see Dr Munro on board the steamer in Kessock roads – evening remarkably fine.

March 15: Attended a meeting of the committee for building new Chapel, etc., etc. Day uncommonly fine.

March 16: Attended Mrs Sherriff's funeral and read the burial office. The weather has suddenly changed into a regular storm, blowing all day from the east, and snowing without intermission; prepared sermon for Sunday.

March 17 (Sunday): Weather uncommonly cold; Chapel consequently thinly attended; preached twice on the Transfiguration.

March 18: Transacted some important business connected with the new Chapel; attended meeting about the Maggot *[near present-day Friars' Bridge where the Church had land from which they received feus]*; wrote an official letter to Bp. Low regarding the state of the Diocese, and some other letters on Church affairs.

March 19: Engaged a good part of the forenoon about the new Chapel, and the settlement of the Maggot business. Day rather fine, but still cold.

March 20: After public prayers, made some calls and afterwards walked out to Ness Cottage, and spent the evening, and returned home about 10.

March 21: Engaged in the forenoon chiefly about New Chapel, and consulting about settlement with tenants on the Maggot; weather very cold, and a deal of snow fell on the evening; saw sowing of oats for the first time in the season.

March 22: Weather still cold and squally; engaged in the forenoon with Mr *[William]* Robertson *[Elgin]*, the architect; morning and evening as usual with the children; Mrs F. confined to bed all day with a cold.

March 23: Nothing occurred worthy of remark; dined at Mr G. Anderson's and prepared a new circular for getting additional subscriptions to the Chapel; returned home early and finished my preparations for Sunday.

March 24 (Sunday): The Chapel rather full in the forenoon and very thin in the evening in consequence of the severity of the weather; a great deal of snow fell during the day with cold north-east wind. Preached in the forenoon on the Institution of the Lord's Supper, and in the evening on the 53rd chapter of Isaiah.

March 25: Nothing occurred worthy of remark; weather still continues cold with occasional showers of snow.

March 26: Nothing occurred worthy of remark; weather still very cold.

March 27: After public prayers made several professional visits; spent the remainder of the day as usual. Mrs F. confined with a bad cold.

March 28: Nothing occurred worthy of notice (weather cold).

March 29 (Good Friday): The congregation rather numerous and the service altogether very satisfactory – music very good – voluntary particularly beautiful (subject "He was despised and rejected") – great and marked attention to the sermon. Mrs F. still confined by her cold. Saw baby Munro for the first time after her illness; after service made some professional calls.

March 30: After Prayers in Chapel visited some young people who were to be communicants for the first time; made arrangements for the services of the Festival, and had a long practising of the singers. Mrs F. still confined by her cold.

March 31 (Easter Day): A very good congregation – <u>seventy-two</u> communicants – the service on the whole very satisfactory – a little jarring in the musical department in one or two instances (nothing particular).

April 1: After Prayers in the Chapel made several calls.

April 2: Nothing particular occurred, wrote several letters in the evening applying for additional subscriptions to the new Chapel.

April 3: Went to the Infirmary to see Mrs Alex. Mackay who had her leg broken by a fall. Afterwards administered sacrament to a sick person. This day has been <u>bitterly</u> cold, with frosty wind from the south-east.

April 4: Weather continues remarkably cold, nothing particular occurred; wrote some letters about the new Chapel.

April 5: Weather much the same; wrote a letter to Mr J. Mackenzie *[banker]* about *[the]* sale of the old Chapel *[the start of an acrimonious correspondence – see Appendix, page 121]*.

April 6: Dined at Muirtown to meet Capt. Mackenzie, Mountgerald *[north-east of Dingwall]*. Mrs Fyvie and I walked home in the evening.

April 7 (Sunday): A fine day and a tolerably full Chapel both forenoon and afternoon; the singing remarkably good.

April 8: Nothing occurred worthy of notice; weather cold and dry.

April 9: Nothing occurred worthy of notice; weather still very cold and no appearance of vegetation.

April 10: Do.   do.,   as yesterday

April 11: Went to Fortrose to read the burial office over the remains of Mr Clarke's infant. Mrs F. went along with me; the weather suddenly changed and became quite warm.

April 12 (Mrs F.'s birthday): Soft and warm; dined at Mrs Fraser's, Ness Cottage, with a large party. Walked home at night and joined Mrs. F. at Dr Munro's.

April 13: Wrote a sermon on the character of Balaam *[a diviner/prophet in the Book of Numbers]*; attended practising; made some calls and wrote a letter *[?to]* Munro in London.

April 14 (Sunday): Chapel pretty full, and weather mild; the services on the whole satisfactory; singing good. In the evening read part of vol. VI of Bingham on the style of preaching in the early Church, etc., etc.

April 15: Received a letter from Miss Walker of Huntly intimating her father's illness *[Rev. James Walker, incumbent at Huntly, 1781 –1842; Dean of Moray, 1829 –1839 or 1842]*; also one from Mr Archibald Dunbar about Capt. Sherriff's appointment in India; called on Mrs Warrand at Muirtown.

April 16: Weather very dry, but warmer; scarcely any appearance of vegetation; unpleasant correspondence with Mr Mackenzie, Banker.

April 17: Made several calls in forenoon; read the current number of "London Quarterly Review" – an excellent article on Oxford Theology.

April 18: Cold with occasional showers of hail, walked to Muirtown with Mrs F. and all the children. Letter from Mr Bowdler about New*[?]* Chapel. Began to read "Life of Wilberforce" *[5-volume biography by his sons, published 1838]*.

April 19: Continued reading "Life of Wilberforce"; disagreeable correspondence with Mr J. Mackenzie.

April 20: Practising; weather gradually becoming milder, but little vegetation. Still reading "Wilberforce"; made preparations for Sunday, etc.

April 21 (Sunday): Day fine and Chapel rather full; services very satisfactory; music capital. After evening service heard that Lord Ward *[William Ward, 1st Earl of Dudley]* had been in Chapel at both services – had remarked his devout manner, not knowing who he was.

April 22: Occupied most of the day in helping Mrs Munro in making arrangements for her departure for London; sat up till the arrival of the mail, and no letter from Dr Munro.

April 23: Got up at 4 and accompanied Mrs Munro to Cromarty just in time to meet the steamer; saw her safely on board with her baby *[born May 1836]*, and then returned to Inverness. Day uncommonly fine, and drive from Cromarty to Fortrose very beautiful and interesting. Much provoked by J. Mc's conduct.

April 24: Disagreeable correspondence with J. M., very sad and irritating; reading "Life of Wilberforce" and greatly delighted and trust edified by it. Matilda Fraser dined; beautiful evening.

April 25: Letter from Dr Munro, addressed to Mrs Munro, by which knew that he was well; weather mild with occasional showers. Still reading "Wilberforce".

April 26: Day very fine, vegetation advancing rapidly; read third volume of "Wilberforce" – ludicrous anecdote about the old Earl of Bridgewater calling Bp. *[Beilby]* Porteous *[Bishop of Chester and then of London]* "that confounded Presbyterian", because he had voted against him about some casual*[?]* bill.

April 27: Reading "Life of Wilberforce"; correspondence with J. M. I hope ended; wrote several letters; weather now very fine. Nothing particular occurred. A good practising of choir, greatly improved – a great source of enjoyment to me.

April 28 (Sunday): Lord Ward again in Chapel in the afternoon; called on him afterwards and got £10 for New Chapel; very pleasant, nice fellow. Service satisfactory; music capital, and sermons I hope attentively and profitably heard.

April 29: Meeting of committee for building Chapel; authority obtained for raising a loan on old Chapel. Letter from Dr Munro very kind and good and intimated safe arrival of Mrs M. and baby in

London. Vexatious conduct of J. M. – thought *sursum corda [Lift up your hearts]* would make a good motto for a seal with some device to correspond. Reading last vol. of Wilberforce's life – much impressed upon the whole with the character of Wilberforce – a good man certainly and deeply imbued with the spirit of religion, and "the mind it was in Christ Jesus". Shall always recommend it.

April 30: Day rather wasted in the forenoon on business appointments or rather disappointments; in the evening read last volume of "Wilberforce". Mem: He says "Any one whom I love at all I seem to love better in a land of mountains". Never was saying more true. Query: what is the cause of this? Is it because nature great and we little? Wilberforce makes use of the term "bird-witted" which seems very expressive. My admiration of Wilberforce's character still increasing and I hope I have profited by the book which I have nearly finished.

May 1: Weather quite hot; did some business in the early part of the day, and called at Ness Cottage on the way home. In the evening finished the "Life of Wilberforce" – highly useful and edifying. The Duke of Wellington's birthday. Heard that Mrs R. Sherriff *(Jane Duff)* had had a son on 22nd December.

May 2: Nothing particular occurred; weather warm and beautiful.

May 3: Dined at Muirtown to meet the Misses Mackenzie, Mountgerald. Walked home in the evening; some delightful showers, and fields beginning to look quite green.

May 4: A letter from Admiral Duff offering Mrs Fyvie a settlement of £150 a year, on condition that we stop legal proceedings, which accepted cheerfully.

May 5 (Sunday): Rainy and cold, chapel uncommonly thinly attended; music capital.

May 6: Transacted some business and made several calls; day very fine; nothing particular occurred; in the evening wrote to Mr Ramsay, and sent a copy of Lady Rosse's trust.

(The Countess of Rosse, who died in January 1838, left a sum of £6000, the annual proceeds of which were to be applied towards erecting Episcopal chapels and assisting in the education of young men for the Episcopal Church, preference to be given to the Highlands and Highlanders, and Dean Fyvie was appointed one of the trustees of the fund.) [The Rosse title is that of an Irish peerage.]

May 7: Spent most of day in town; Mr Sheppard's sale *[deceased*

Town Clerk]; letter from Admiral Duff, all quite satisfactory.

May 8: Nothing particular occurred; weather warm and showery, and country looking beautiful.

May 9: Day cold, with occasional showers of hailstones. Mr Warrand dined with us. The Miss Frasers and young friend from Dalvey came to tea. Prayers in Chapel, being Ascension Day, very ill attended.

May 10: Nothing particular occurred; finished half of first volume of Lord Lindsay's "Letters from the Holy Land" *["Letters on Egypt, Edom and the Holy Land", published 1838 – Edom was an area south of the Dead Sea]* and much pleased. How much I should like to visit Egypt, etc., etc.

May 11: Nothing particular occurred; received an excellent letter from Mrs R. Macfarlane; proceeding with L*[ord]* L*[indsay]*'s "Letters"; prepared sermons for Sunday. Heard of resignation of Lord Melbourne and his Ministry. What a happy riddance of evil counsellors from about the Throne of this great Empire.

[Melbourne was out of office only briefly, as Robert Peel refused to form a government unless Queen Victoria dismissed some of the wives and daughters of Whig MPs who made up her entourage: this event is called the 'Bedchamber Crisis'. Melbourne was persuaded to stay on as Prime Minister.]

May 12 (Sunday): Chapel rather thinly attended; preached on the subject of the Ascension, a.m. and p.m.

May 13: Weather suddenly changed and become very cold, wind blowing from the north-east with occasional showers of snow.

May 14: Snow lying on the ground all day and looking quite like February; finished Lord Lindsay's "Letters".

May 15: Rain from north-east all day, and very cold; nothing particular occurred.

May 16: Day a little milder; nothing particular occurred.

May 17: Went to board the London steamer and had an interview with Mr Oldfield. Mrs Munro and baby returned from London. N.B.: baptised twin children in Margaret Street.

May 18: Made preparation for Sunday; calls, etc.; nothing particular.

May 19 (Whitsunday): A fine day; Chapel nearly full; there were 56 communicants; the service altogether very satisfactory; music still improving; preached forenoon and afternoon.

May 20: After Prayers in Chapel walked to Muirtown to call for Mrs Warrand; new Chapel becoming quite beautiful.

May 21: Began to teach the two Macraes, *[James]* Kent's anthem "Hear my Prayer" *[scored for two soprano soloists plus chorus]*. Nothing particular occurred; reading Knox for the third time.

May 22: In the new Chapel most of the forenoon, making arrangements about putting in the stained glass in the Altar window. Reading Knox and the sixth volume of Bingham; weather fine.

May 23: Engaged again about Altar window for some hours in the forenoon. Reading Bingham; weather fine.

May 24: Reading Knox and sixth volume of Bingham. Weather warm and natural. Mrs Macpherson and Matilda Fraser dined with us; late walk.

May 25: Had accounts of the death of poor Harriet Bowdler, who had scarcely been ten months married to Rev. William Pinder; what a sad blow to all that excellent family. Mr Bowdler's letter written with wonderful resignation, and in a true Christian spirit. How I pity poor Mr Pinder. I can scarce imagine any affliction greater than his, nothing but the deepest inward religion could support a man under such a trial.

May 26 (Trinity Sunday): Preached twice on subjects appropriate to the day. Chapel rather full. In the evening finished 6th vol. of Bingham, which like the rest, is very valuable in the establishment of facts connected with ecclesiastical practice. Calvin was a strenuous advocate for <u>weekly</u>, or at least <u>monthly</u>, Communions, but could not succeed in establishing them at Geneva. Communions <u>once</u> a year of Popish origin entirely. Mem.: Curious notice of what was called "Dry Masses" first used on board ship, i.e., the service of the mass without the distribution of the elements.

May 27: Nothing particular occurred worth noting.

May 28: Ditto.   ditto.,   weather fine

May 29: Most of the forenoon in town variously occupied; dined early. Mr D*[uncan]* Mackenzie called in the evening on his way to Strathnairn; gave him £5 from Lady Rosse's Fund for his Catechist and poor people. Afterwards walked up with him to the top of Leys; fine night but wind easterly.

May 30: Called at Ness Cottage on my way to town; nothing particular occurred during the day.

39

May 31: Altar window quite finished; nothing particular.

June 1: Wrote a sermon on the Love of God from the Epistle for the Sunday, and made usual preparations for the Sunday services.

June 2 (Sunday): Fine day. Chapel almost full; service satisfactory and music very good and steady; a considerable number of strangers in Church both forenoon and afternoon.

June 3: Perfect summer weather; watering the garden in the evening. Pease in blossom, spinnage *[spinach]* for the first time in the season; reading 7th volume of Bingham.

June 4: Weather very hot and dry; nothing occurred worthy of notice.

June 5: Still very dry and hot; in the evening M. Fraser and E. Dunbar called to take leave before going to Burghead for sea bathing; walked home with them to Ness Cottage.

June 6: Most delicious showers and the air quite warm and balmy; the face of nature quite refreshed and delightful.

June 7: Weather most beautiful, soft and warm; made several forenoon visits to members of the congregation; after tea and lessons, wrought in the garden; afterwards read one of Mr Newman's sermons.

June 8: Day, deliciously summer; good practising in Chapel; made some calls in forenoon; preparing for Sunday as usual, but did not compose a sermon this week.

June 9 (Sunday): Upon the whole the day was very pleasing; Chapel very full and congregation attentive; a new sett *[set, or perhaps, setting]* of chants in the evening, very well sung. Perfect summer.

June 10: At home most of the day superintending some work in the garden; some fine refreshing rain in the evening. Reading Knox (not John) and Bingham by turns.

June 11: Nothing particular occurred throughout the day.

June 12: Nothing particular occurred.

June 13: Baptised a child in the forenoon, and made several calls; weather very hot.

June 14: Mrs F. and I went to call at Daviot and Farr. At Farr saw Rev. J*[oseph]* Eaton of Chester; spent the day there and returned home in the evening by the west road; day quite beautiful, perfect summer.

June 15: Nothing particular occurred; weather uncommonly fine. Had a letter from Mr Walker of Huntly, announcing the death of his son William.

June 16 (Sunday – 3 Trinity): Day extremely hot; Chapel pretty full and attentive congregation, I hope profitably so; the singing was <u>excellent</u> – Heathcot*[e]*'s *Magnificat* in the evening – a most beautiful chant.

June 17: Mrs F. and I and Maggy went to Burghead – by the "Star" coach as far as Forres and onwards three miles, then walked to Burghead and joined Mrs Fraser (Ness Cottage) and family party. Day delightful, bright and warm with south wind.

June 18: Excessive heat – thermometer at 78°*[F; 26°C]* in shade, walked about the seaside in the forenoon and rowed out to the steamer to receive Mrs Macpherson and her boys; in the evening went to Duffus with Maggy and left her with her grandmother.

June 19: Had rained heavily (with thunder) during the night; morning quite delicious; bathed in the open sea before breakfast; dined at Mr Sutherland's and met Mr Maclaren *[probably the incumbent, Elgin, 1837–1859; also Maclauren and Maclaurin]*; showery and warm.

June 20: Drove to Elgin in Mr Sutherland's gig; made various calls; took Mr Maclaren back to Burghead, where dined with Mr Fraser's family and walked out in the evening.

June 21: Bathed before breakfast, Mr Maclaren ditto. After breakfast Mr Maclaren left for Elgin and Mrs F., Maggy and I set out for Forres on our way to Inverness. Miss Matilda Fraser accompanied us as far *[as]* Kinloss, but the day being rainy was obliged to stop there; joined the "Defiance" coach at Forres and arrived safely at Roseheath at quarter past seven and found all well. Rain most of the day without intermission.

June 22: Nothing particular occurred; the day soft and mild. Unexpected renewal of unpleasant correspondence with Mr J. Mackenzie.

June 23 (Sunday): Day very rainy. Rev. E. Eaton of St. Mary's, Chester, preached forenoon and afternoon. He and Capt. Mackintosh of Farr, sister, etc., E. Mackintosh, Mrs Troughton, dined at Roseheath. *[and][?]* G. and P. Anderson.

June 24: Nothing particular occurred.

June 25: Nothing particular occurred.

June 26: Day cool but pleasant, received and wrote several letters; heard of the death of Capt. A. Macpherson and went to visit his widow.

June 27: Thursday before the sacrament in the Kirk – the fast as they call it (lucus a non lucendo) *[= it is a grove by not being light, i.e. an absurd statement]*. At home all day and enjoyed the quiet much; out in the garden with the children making desperate efforts to demolish the caterpillars, made tremendous havock among the enemy with the aid of a new besom and a sheet to receive the fallen or wounded; bushes lost for the season.

June 28: Day damp and cold; read the burial service over the remains of Capt. A. Macpherson; made some calls afterwards and returned home early; in the evening reading and lessons as usual.

June 29: Made calls and attended practising of choir; dined at Mr G. Anderson's to meet Mr Dorcey from Glasgow *[probably A. J. D. D'Orsey, teacher at Glasgow High School, who later became an Episcopalian priest in Anderston, Glasgow]*. Received a very interesting letter from Hon. James Sinclair about forming an Episcopal Congregation at Wick.

June 30 (Sunday): A good many strangers in Church; the weather quite beautiful, nothing particular in the services.

July 1: Weather uncommonly fine, nothing particular occurred.

July 2: Do.   Do.   Attended D'Orsey's lectures.

July 3: Do.   Do.   Do.

July 4: Nothing particular occurred.

July 5: Miss Fraser from Aberdeen dined with us – a very delightful person – fine specimen of Christian old age, cheerful and animated, gentle and obliging, with sterling right principles. Matilda and Alick Fraser came to tea – walked to town with Miss Fraser and afterwards part of the way to Ness Cottage; rather cold, and wind very high.

July 6: Attended practising, and made several professional calls.

July 7 (Sunday, 6 Trinity): Day very warm and Chapel very full both forenoon and afternoon; intend to set out tomorrow by "Defiance" *[coach]* to Aberdeen to attend biennial meeting.

July 8: Went to Aberdeen by the "Defiance" coach; took up Mr Dunbar at Elgin; very pleasant journey, and weather delightful.

July 9: Attended meeting of committee of Friendly Society and afterwards dinner at Bishop Skinner's with a considerable number of clergy – a very pleasant day.

[Bishop William Skinner was Bishop of Aberdeen from 1816 to 1857, and Primus from 1841 to 1857; he was the son of Bishop John Skinner who was Bishop from 1786 to 1816, and Primus from 1788 to 1816.]

July 10: Meeting of Friendly Society; business all smooth and everything conducted with great propriety; dined with the clergy as usual at the Inn.

July 11: Attended meeting of Church Society, and heard detail of proceedings from Mr Ramsay – left at 3 o'clock for Huntly and arrived there at 8 o'clock p.m.

July 12: Spent a very agreeable evening and slept at Mr Walker's; got up early and looked at his chapel, etc.; left per mail at 12 and arrived at Inverness at 7 p.m. and found all well. Day rainy throughout.

July 13: Soft and beautiful with occasional showers; called at Ness Cottage on my way to town; found that Mr J. Mackenzie had printed and circulated my correspondence with him about the Chapel. *["Correspondence betwixt John Mackenzie, Esq. Banker, Inverness, and the Revd. Charles Fyvie, relative to the Episcopal Chapel in Inverness", published by R. Carruthers, 1839 – see appendix, page 121.]* Attended practising, etc.

July 14 (Sunday): Day beautiful, and Chapel quite full forenoon and afternoon. Unexpected appearance of Mr Morgan. Mrs F. played the organ – singing beautiful, more and more dulcified with Heathcote's chant to the "Magnificat". Mr Morgan and Mr and Mrs G. Anderson drank tea with us.

July 15: Rained heavily most of the forenoon; drank tea at Raigmore's and took Mr Morgan along with us.

July 16: A beautiful day; spent the forepart of the day much as usual; dined at Raigmore's and had a good deal of interesting conversation on religious subjects with the Ladies.

July 17: Nothing occurred worthy of notice; weather perfect; had potatoes for the first time for the season; pease sometime ago.

July 18: Nothing particular occurred.

July 19: Nothing particular occurred; Mrs F. and I drank tea at Mr

Macpherson's at Heath Cottage; delightful walk home.

July 20: Long practising of choir; went in the evening to Mrs Fraser's, Ness Cottage; perfect summer weather.

July 21 (Sunday, 8 Trinity): Chapel nearly full; day beautiful; service satisfactory, but nothing unusual occurred.

July 22: Engaged in the new Chapel all forenoon, and dined in the evening at Heath Cottage and met Capt. *[later Major, then Colonel]* Greenwood of the Royal Artillery.

July 23: Made several professional calls in the forenoon and spent the evening at home as usual; weather beautiful.

July 24: Waited the arrival of Bishop Low and Mr Williams at Muirtown Locks – very late – wet night.

July 25: Spent the early part of the day with Bp. Low and Mr Williams, visited the new Chapel; walked about the town with Mrs F., Mr Williams, Mrs Greenhill and Miss Codrington. Saw the Bp. and Mr Williams across Kessock Ferry; returned to dinner – Matilda Fraser dined with us; walked to Ness Cottage with her in the evening.

July 26: Beautiful day; went to town early in hopes of finding Dr Faussett and Mr Lumsdaine at the Inn, but found they had gone; comforted myself by spending some hours in assisting the glazier in fitting the muslin blinds to the upper lights in new Chapel. Vexed and mortified about J. M.'s conduct in persevering to torment me – "We count them happy who endure." *[James v.11]*

July 27: Weather uncommonly hot; went to town early to meet Bp. Low and Mr Williams on their return from Allangrange; saw them off again for Highfield. Had an explanation with the Bp. about J. M.'s conduct to me; attended practising and returned home early to dinner.

July 28 (Sunday): Communion Sunday (9 Trinity); Chapel full but fewer communicants that usual (42). Weather exceedingly warm.

July 29: Nothing particular occurred.

July 30: Made several official calls in the morning; went to Heath Cottage to tea to meet Mr Burke.

July 31: Day wet and rather cold easterly wind; partly expected Mr Williams to dinner on his way from Dingwall to Aberdeen, but found he had passed through without stopping. Finished reading Harcourt on "The Deluge" *[Leveson Venables Vernon-Harcourt: "The doctrine of the deluge: vindicating the Scriptural account from the doubts which have recently been cast upon it by geological speculations" (1838)]*, a curious book not interesting enough to reward the trouble of perusal, except to antiquarians, strictly so called; there seems something in his Ark theory, but he wishes to make everything out of it. Wrote to Mr Copeland.

August 1: Nothing particular occurred; weather thoroughly beautiful again.

August 2: Engaged in town during the forenoon, and in the evening had the girls of the choir to get strawberries and cream. Mrs F. had a table and chairs on the green for them.

August 3: Preparation for Sunday; good practising, even their most beautiful. In the evening down by Ness Cottage in hopes of meeting Sir G. Prevost and Miss Prevost on the arrival of the steamboat. Crossed by the islands with Aleck Fraser; went afterwards to Inverness and inquired at the inn, but no arrival.

(Sir George Prevost of Belmont, Hants, was a well-known baronet, who was born in 1804. He was vicar of Stinchcombe, Archdeacon of Gloucester from 1865 to 1880, and died 18th March 1883. His sister, Miss Anne Prevost, so frequently alluded to in Dean Fyvie's diary, used to be a regular visitor to Strathpeffer, and for a time resided in the neighbourhood of Dingwall, where she took an active interest in the Episcopal congregation, under the incumbency of Rev. W. J. Bussel [1859–1889]. Miss Prevost died on 12th November 1882.)

August 4 (Sunday): Very beautiful day and Chapel full. Rev. Henry Melville *[London, and from 1843 Principal of the East India College, Haileybury]* there – had no opportunity of speaking to him. Dined with Mr G. Anderson and walked to the ferry in hopes of meeting Bishop Low, but found he would not arrive till Monday.

August 5: Met Bishop at Kessock Ferry; after spending some time in town we walked to Roseheath in time to dinner; a very few friends dined.

August 6: Set out with the Bishop and Mrs F. in a phæton for Elgin; took the Culloden Moor road and called on Mrs Campbell at Kilravock Castle; dined there and then proceeded by Cawdor Castle as far as Forres where we stopped all night. The grounds at Kilravock magnificent.

August 7: Breakfasted at Forres and afterwards proceeded to Elgin under very heavy rain. Dined with the Morayshire clergy at Mr Maclauren's *[also Maclaurin – incumbent, Elgin, 1837–1859]*, and slept at Sir A. Dunbar's *[Sir Archibald Dunbar, 6th Bart, of Northfield, Duffus House, 1772–1849]*.

August 8: Day of the visitation. Mr Williams read prayers, Mr Maclauren preached and Rev. Bp. charged *[i.e. gave his words of guidance to the clergy]*. All very well. Clergy dined together after the business of the day was over; made some calls in Elgin after dinner.

August 9: Started from Sir A. Dunbar's with Mrs F. at 10 o'clock for Inverness – day delightful, dined at Kilravock Castle and walked over the grounds with increased astonishment; nothing I have ever seen half so beautiful; reached home at 11 – all well (D.G.).

August 10: Usual occupation of the Saturday with no incidents; distressed with an inflamed eye.

August 11 (Sunday): Day beautiful and Chapel very full. Mr Troughton read prayers in the morning – my eye still very painful – preached twice with difficulty. Miss Prevost in Church; walked with her and Miss Shaw to their lodging after evening service.

August 12: Miss Prevost and Miss Shaw dined with us; Matilda and Alex Fraser to tea – very pleasant day.

August 13: Called for Miss Prevost in the forenoon and afterwards dined at Muirtown – Huntly Duff had arrived from England – looked in good health – came home early.

August 14: Nothing particular occurred; day rather cold and wet.

August 15: Called early at Ness Cottage and walked into town with Matilda; joined Mrs Fyvie and called for Miss Prevost; walked out with Miss Shaw; day cold with northerly wind.

August 16: Drove with Miss Prevost, Miss Shaw and Matilda Fraser to Culloden Muir and Clava, Ness Castle, Ness Cottage, etc., and afterwards dined at Raigmore's. († day) On crossing the crazy wooden bridge across the River Nairn at Clava, Miss Prevost told me an anecdote which I here note down. "Her (Miss Prevost's) grandaunt was a maid of honour to the Princess Amelia, sister to William, Duke of Cumberland, of Culloden memory. She had engaged herself in marriage to Mr Macleod (then of Rasay) and on opening the subject to the Princess, she was very much annoyed at loosing the personal attendance of her friend, and said: 'Pray, who are you to be married to?' The lady replied 'To a Scotchman.' The Princess Amelia said with some indignation: 'A Scotchman! And what may his name be?' The reply was Macleod of Highland Boath *[sic]*. On hearing this, the Princess said with great vehemence 'I

46

thought my brother <u>William</u> had extirpated all <u>that</u> ~~whole~~ <u>race</u>.' "

(Lieut.-General Sir George Prevost, 1st Bart., of the 60th Regiment, and Commander of the Forces in British North America, married Catherine Ann, daughter of Major-General John Phipps, by Jane Macleod, his wife, sister of Lieut.-General Sir John Macleod, G.C.H.)

August 17: Death and funeral of Mr P*[aul]* Maccoll *[formerly incumbent, Appin/Ballachulish]*; very distressing circumstances – quite worn out with fatigue; tea at Ness Cottage with Miss Prevost; afterwards to Muirtown to bring Mrs F. home.

August 18 (Sunday): Mr Troughton preached in the forenoon. In the afternoon Mr Smith from Northhampton read prayers and I preached. Chapel very full – an interesting day and weather delightful.

August 19: Accompanied Miss Prevost and her friend to the Falls of Kilmorack, etc. and parted with them at Beauly, on their way to the Isle of Skye. I returned to Inverness in Mr Cumming's gig; felt not at all well the whole day.

August 20: Confined to bed to noon; beautiful day, walked to town and was there for an hour or so; came home, dined early, and read Lord Mahon's "History of England" *[probably "History of England from the Peace of Utrecht to the Peace of Aix-la-Chapelle" (1836)]*.

August 21: Wrote several letters to friends and on business; continued to read Lord Mahon's "History"; went to the new Chapel with Eneas and Julia Mackintosh of Raigmore, in the forenoon; beautiful harvest weather, and harvest commenced in all directions round us.

August 22: Nothing particular occurred during the day. Mr Warrand, Huntly Duff, Eneas Mackintosh, etc., etc., dined with us; a pleasant day.

August 23: Called at Ness Castle to see Lady Saltoun *[probably the wife of Alexander Fraser, 17th Lord Saltoun]*; went with her to the new Chapel, where she chose a seat in the gallery. Weather beautiful and harvest becoming general.

August 24: Nothing particular occurred.

August 25 (Sunday): Chapel very full. Mr Troughton read prayers in the morning; nothing particular occurred in connection with the duties of the day. I announced a collection for the Episcopal Church Society to be made Sunday next. At half-past nine in the evening called away unexpectedly to baptise a dying infant (Mr Pearson's).

August 26: Nothing particular occurred; reading Lister's "Life of Clarendon" *[Thomas Henry Lister, 1838]* – a very unpleasant book – the author seems quite incapable of appreciating Charles the First's character. *[Clarendon was an informal advisor to Charles I and later chief advisor to Charles II.]*

August 27: Read the burial office over the child I had baptised on Sunday night; much occupied in the new Chapel rest of the day; dined at Viewmount *[Dr Munro's]* and came home early. († day)

August 28: Married the Rev. James Paterson in St. John's Chapel. Day rainy and cold; spent two hours in the new Chapel and returned home at 3 o'clock to begin a sermon for the next Sunday.

August 29: Day rainy for the most part; went for a little to hear Dr Chalmers on the subject of Kirk extension – was disappointed in his eloquence, and his views not deeply grounded. The Presbyterian schism seems to have lived out nearly its appointed time as a British establishment. *[Dr Thomas Chalmers was to become the leader of the Great Disruption of 1843 in the Church of Scotland, which led to the establishment of the Free Church of Scotland. He gave two lectures in Inverness as part of a Highland tour.]*

August 30: Preparing discourses for Sunday with reference to the Episcopal Church Society; day pleasant with slight showers occasionally; nothing particular occurred.

August 31: Busy most of the day with my sermon for the Episcopal Church Society; attended practising and visited Mr Hunter who is thought to be in a dying state.

September 1 (Sunday): Chapel full; Mr Troughton read prayers. I preached for the Society – the collection amounted to £37 which was very handsome. Mr Troughton preached in the afternoon.

September 2: Went to town early and called for Miss Prevost who had arrived from Skye on Saturday; spent some time in the Chapel and visited Mr Hunter again, and made several calls. Miss Prevost and her friend came up to Roseheath in the evening with the intention of remaining with us a week.

September 3: Visited Mr Hunter again; and made several professional calls in the forenoon.

September 4: Nothing particular happened; saw Mr Hunter and administered the Holy Sacrament to him. Miss P. unwell and not able to go out.

September 5: Made several professional visits. Matilda Fraser came to dinner and Mr Macpherson to tea. Reading Lister's "Life of Clarendon", almost against my own will.(† day)

September 6: Married Alexr. Macrae to Miss Maclarty; visited some sick people; weather most beautiful and harvest in progress. (†)

September 7: Nothing particular occurred; some heavy showers but sunshine predominating.

September 8 (Sunday): Beautifully filled Chapel forenoon and afternoon; performed the whole duty without any assistance, Mr Troughton officiating at Strathnairn; day upon the whole very satisfactory.

September 9: Called at Ness Cottage on my way to town; spent a considerable part of the forenoon in new Chapel; evening at home occupied as usual. Miss Prevost still with us.

September 10: Drove out with Miss Prevost as far as Aldourie; afterwards she and Miss Shaw went to Inverness to remain in a lodging for a fortnight.

September 11: Day uncommonly beautiful. In the forenoon Rev. J. Brown of Leeds, one of Dr Hook's curates, called with a note from Dr. Hook *[Walter Farquhar Hook, Vicar of Leeds, 1837–1859, and then Dean of Chichester]*. Showed him the way to Culloden Moor and appointed to meet him afterwards in the new Chapel; dined with us in the evening, Miss Banyon and Alex Fraser, Ness Cottage, to meet him.

September 12: Occupied most of the forenoon in the new Chapel; nothing particular occurred; beautiful harvest weather.

September 13: Engaged all day in the new Chapel; anxious to forward the work to have it opened on the 30th of this month; at night began a sermon for Sunday.

September 14: Most of the forenoon about the new Chapel; made trial of the singing for the first time and found the effect beautiful; at night finished my sermon.

September 15 (Sunday): A regular storm of wind and rain from the east, very few in Church and none from the country except Mackintosh; a really melancholy, dismal day. Mr Troughton read prayers in the morning, and I preached from the text "Have salt in yourselves and have peace one to another" *[Mark ix.50]*.

September 16: All last night blew a perfect hurricane from the east, much damage done; today rather fine but the ground thoroughly soaked with rain. Occupied most of the day in forwarding the work in the new Chapel.

September 17: A fine day; wrote several letters chiefly to clerical brethren; engaged much as usual.

September 18: Ditto, ditto; nothing particular occurred.

September 19: Ditto, ditto; in new Chapel most of the day; went out for an hour to make professional calls.

September 20: Mrs Troughton, Mr Troughton and Mr Mackintosh, Daviot, and a few friends dined with us.

September 21: Nothing particular occurred beyond the usual duties of Saturday; a very beautiful harvest day.

September 22 (Sunday): Mr Troughton preached in the morning and read prayers in the afternoon. After the sermon in the morning I publicly announced the opening of the new Chapel on Sunday next. The day mild and beautiful, and the Chapel very full – "like the valleys thick set with corn" [misquoted from Psalm lxv.13].

September 23: Had the organ removed from the old Chapel; at new Chapel the whole day.

September 24: All day again at new Chapel, organ nearly put up and work going forward satisfactorily; nearly all the congregation accommodated to their minds with pews.

September 25: Busy in getting forward the work in the new Chapel; had the organ in a state to be played.

September 26: Occupied the whole day in new Chapel.

September 27: Ditto; in the evening Mr [William C.] Maclauren [incumbent, Elgin, 1837–1850] and Mr [Charles] Bigsby [incumbent, Fochabers, 1836–1840] arrived; dined at Mr G. Anderson's.

September 28: With great exertion got the new Chapel in a fit state to be opened on Sunday (Michaelmas Day). Mr [Alexander] Bruce of Banff [incumbent, 1815–1862] arrived. The Clergy dined with us, or rather with Mrs F. for I was not able to get away from the Chapel till 8 o'clock. Miss Prevost, Miss Shaw and Mr G. Anderson also dined. (Mr McLauren's anecdote about Bishop Magendie's having been consulted as to whether a Clergyman could marry himself, said "Can you bury yourself?").

September 29 (Sunday, St. Michael's): New Chapel opened. Rev. W. C. McLauren preached in the morning [from Genesis xxxii.29], and Rev. C. Bigsby in the afternoon *[from Psalm lxxxiv.4-7 – see "Inverness Courier" for 5th October]*. I read the Communion Service and pronounced the blessing. Rev. A. Bruce, Banff, read the Epistle. A most pleasing day – all smooth and no mistake, and a splendid congregation. The collection at the door amounted to £30 4s 6d.

September 30: Dined at Mr G. Anderson's with Mr Bruce and Mr Maclauren; walked home late by beautiful moonlight, and had a deal of interesting conversation.

October 1: Mr Maclauren left; nothing particular occurred.

October 2: Went to Falls of Foyers with Miss Prevost; snow on *[Ben]* Wyvies *[sic]* in the morning.

October 3: Great cattle show *[held by the Highland Society in the Academy park on 3rd and 4th October – see "Inverness Courier" for 5th October]*.

October 4: Went with Miss Prevost to the competition of pipers in the Pavilion; striking enough sight.

October 5: Nothing particular occurred; preparing for Sunday.

October 6 (Sunday): Did all the duty myself, and ministered the sacrament to 56 persons; a good congregation and service satisfactory.

October 7: Nothing particular occurred.

October 8: Went to Elgin with Miss Prevost.

October 9: Slept at Mr Maclauren's and breakfasted today; walked Elgin – in the Cathedral, etc. with Miss Prevost; took leave of her and Miss Shaw at 2 o'clock, and returned to Inverness by the "Defiance" coach, in time to dine at Kingsmills.

October 10: The whole day in the new Chapel.

October 11: Ditto, ditto, arranging about the Pulpit and Desk.

October 12: Ditto, ditto, ditto; called at Ness Cottage on my way to town, and walked in with Mrs Fraser – very sorry to learn their loss of income.

October 13 (Sunday): A beautiful day and a good congregation; forenoon sermon from "Thou God seest me" *[Gen. xvi.13]*, most attentively and I hope profitably listened to; new Chapel gradually getting into proper order.

October 14: A beautiful day; drove out with Mrs F. to call on Mr *[William Fraser]* Tytler's *[local Sheriff]* family at Aldourie; dined afterwards at Ness Cottage, and walked home at night.

October 15: In the new Chapel the greater part of the forenoon; Matilda and Alex Fraser dined with us.

October 16: Nothing particular occurred; much occupied about arrangements in the Chapel.

October 17: In Chapel the whole forenoon; nothing particular occurred worthy of notice.

October 18: Most beautiful weather; walked into town via Ness Cottage.

October 19: Weather quite summer-like; composed a sermon for Sunday; attended practising, etc., etc.

October 20 (Sunday): Fine congregation both in the morning and afternoon; much encouragement for new Chapel.

October 21: A beautiful day with rather high wind; Mrs Fraser, Matilda and Alexr. dined; also Capt. and Miss Macdonald, Kilachonet *[perhaps Kilchoan, Ardnamurchan]*; Helen Munro to tea.

October 22: Usual routine of occupation, a rainy day.

October 23: Ditto, ditto, ditto, and nothing occurred worthy of remark.

October 24: Heavy rain the whole day; about 12 minutes after ten at night a smart shock of an earthquake was distinctly felt here. *[This earthquake was centred near Comrie in Perthshire.]*

October 25: Continued rain, nothing particular occurred.

October 26: Weather cleared up and rather fine; occupied much as usual, with no particular incident.

October 27 (Sunday): Mr Wm. Mackenzie of Muirtown preached forenoon and afternoon. A beautifully filled Chapel, quite cheering to see, some good I hope is doing; a very satisfactory day in all respects.

October 28: Occupied most of the day in making some important alterations about the altar in new Chapel. Read the whole of Price's volume on Providence and Prayers *[part of "Four Dissertations: I. On Providence; II. On Prayer", Richard Price, published 1772]*. Hard frost for the first time.

October 29: Nothing particular occurred; dined at Mr G. Anderson's.

October 30: Nothing particular occurred.

October 31: Variously occupied – alterations in the arrangements of the altar in new Chapel nearly completed.

November 1 (All Saints Day): Called at Muirtown.

November 2: Most of the forenoon in the Chapel; composed a sermon for Sunday on "Examine yourselves whether ye be in the faith", etc. *[2Cor. xiii.5]*; very late to rest.

November 3 (Sunday): I trust a profitable day; sermon very closely attended to; services quite satisfactory, and no jar.

November 4: Nothing particular occurred.

November 5: Very much occupied all day in the Chapel.

November 6: Weather continued very fine; no incident worth recording.

November 7: Beautiful weather but wind easterly.

November 8: Do., do.; occupied most of the day in the Chapel, and in the evening engaged as usual with the boys, and afterwards in preparing a sermon.

November 9: Occupied as usual on Saturdays; at night received intelligence of the death of poor John Anderson *[magistrate, and author of "History of the House of Fraser"]* in the island of St. Vincent; his had been a singular lot.

November 10 (Sunday): A most delightful day; quite like summer; a comfortable day on the whole, but nothing particular.

November 11: Quite summer weather; nothing particular occurred.

November 12: Ditto, ditto, ditto.

November 13: Weather continued beautiful; nothing particular.

November 14: Very much occupied in new Chapel; weather very fine.

November 15: Administered the sacrament to Mr Hunter.

November 16: Occupied as usual on Saturday; nothing particular.

November 17 (Sunday): A beautiful day and Church well filled;

announced Thursday next as a day of thanksgiving for the late plentiful harvest.

November 18: A beautiful day; made several professional calls.

November 19: Received accounts of the death of Col. Macfarlane.

November 20: Weather clear and full of sunshine; very unlike November. Variously occupied – visited Mr Hunter and composed a sermon for the *[Harvest]* Thanksgiving Day.

November 21: Two services for the Thanksgiving; preached in the morning on "The widow of Zarephath" *[1Kings xvii.9-24]*. Weather still equally clear and beautiful.

November 22: Nothing particular occurred.

November 23: Day rather raw and gloomy, with frost towards the evening; occupied as usual on Saturdays.

November 24 (Sunday): A fine day and good congregation; thank God all looks cheering as regards the new Chapel. Received an excellent letter from Mrs R. Macfarlane; dined at Mr Geo. Anderson's and walked home early.

November 25: Sudden change of weather; very hard frost with a good deal of snow falling the whole day.

November 26: Clear sky and very hard frost; beautiful winter day, most strikingly contrasted with the weather we have had hither to, yet very seasonable; called at Ness Cottage.

November 27: Weather much the same; nothing particular occurred; took a long walk in the direction of the Aird.

November 28: Heavy snow most of the day (Martinmas Market).

November 29: Partial thaw, very unpleasant day; nothing of interest.

November 30: As usual on Saturdays, nothing particular occurred.

December 1 (Sunday): A fine clear day with a little frost; a very fair congregation and I hope a profitable day; dined with Mr G. Anderson.

December 2: Fine winter day; no particular occurrence.

December 3: Hard frost; made several professional visits.

December 4: Fine winter day; occupied a good deal about new Chapel; began to make an attempt to teach Sarah to play the organ.

Mem.: first day of 4d postage *[a temporary arrangement, lasting only until 9th January when the penny postage rate was introduced]*.

December 5: Nothing particular occurred.

December 6: Ditto; fine winter weather.

December 7: Ditto, ditto.

December 8 (Sunday): Nothing particular; a fair congregation.

December 9: Called at Mrs Macpherson's, Heath Cottage; a long conversation with her about various things connected with her past and present circumstances.

December 10: Hard frost; made several professional calls and wrote several letters of importance; heard Sarah practice for an hour.

December 11: Matilda Fraser came to Roseheath to remain a few days; hard frost but no snow.

December 12: Walked to Laggan Cottage to call for the Hon. Mr Fraser and his family. The day most beautiful and the country in its winter russet looking really delightful to the eye. Thought I should like to be <u>buried</u> within the new Chapel, between the pulpit and reading desk, in front of the altar.

December 13: Soft, glorious day; nothing of interest occurred.

December 14: Ditto, ditto, ditto.

December 15 (Sunday): Chapel well filled and services very satisfactory; dined at Mr G. Anderson's after evening service, and returned home early.

December 16: Thick fog. Called at Lady Saltoun's and at Ness Cottage.

December 17: Weather fresh and fair; nothing particular occurred.

December 18: Weather much the same; made some professional calls and superintended practising in the Chapel; evening as usual in teaching the children, and reading.

December 19: Nothing particular occurred.

December 20: My Birth day *[sic]* – tempus volat *[= time flies]*

December 21: Composed a sermon for Sunday and otherwise occupied as usual.

December 22 (Sunday): Chapel well filled (heard in the morning that poor Mr Hunter had died at 7 o'clock). Letter from my very dear friend Mr *[Rev. W. J.]* Copeland, Dean of Trinity College, Oxford, which relieved me from much painful anxiety.

December 23: Gloomy December day. New books for the reading desk (the gift of Mrs R. Macfarlane) arrived.

December 24: Rained torrents all day; composed sermon for Christmas under much nervous excitement.

December 25 (Christmas): A very satisfactory day; the services good throughout; a well filled Chapel and 70 communicants (sermon most attentively listened to).

December 26: Hard frost. After prayers in Church read the funeral service over the remains of poor Mr Hunter; a few young people sung a hymn during the time the grave was filling up – the effect was very striking.

December 27: Fine winter day; prayers in Chapel at usual hour.

December 28: Received several interesting letters – from Sir F. Mackenzie, from Mr *[Edward B.]* Ramsay of St. John's, Edinburgh *[incumbent 1830–1872; Dean of Edinburgh 1841–1872, later to publish "Reminiscences of Scottish Life and Character"]*, etc., otherwise as usual on Saturday.

December 29 (Sunday): Chapel tolerably well filled considering the day was very cold; services very attractive.

December 30: Hard frost, very cold, and threatening snow.

December 31: Disagreeable thaw, dark gloomy day (Mr W. Inglis married to Miss C. Gillanders); a very uncomfortable and trying day from various circumstances.

1840

January 1: A fine mild day; service in church as usual but rather thinly attended; spent the evening very quietly at home.

January 2: Went to Nairn Grove to baptise a child of Mr Clarke's; miserably wet, cold, dark day. The Clarkes were remarkably kind, and their infant one of the sweetest creatures I ever baptised. I stood, as its Godfather; let me not forget Amy Clark*[e]*.

January 3: Variously and busily occupied the whole day. Mrs F. had a letter from the widow of her late brother, Col. Macfarlane, previously to his leaving Madras on her homeward voyage. Day miserably wet and gloomy.

January 4: Dark, gloomy day; had a letter from Ld. Ward and from Miss Prevost.

January 5 (Sunday): Cold day with hard frost; made collection for the Infirmary amounting to £14; nothing particular.

January 6: Hard frost, but no snow; attended a public meeting where it was resolved to have a legal assessment for the poor. *[The meeting was held in the High Church, and the proposal had previously been sanctioned by the Town Council and the Kirk Session.]*

January 7: Nothing particular occurred; weather mild and clear. Mrs F. taken very ill during the night.

January 8: Called at Ness Cottage on my way to town; day spent much as usual; two hours in new Chapel.

January 9: Partial thaw; suffering dreadfully from toothache; applied a leech to the gum with some effect; likely to loose a front tooth; unable to do anything until evening.

January 10: Penny Post system began; read Laing's volume on Norway *[Samuel Laing, the elder: "Journal of a Residence in Norway during the years 1834, 1835 and 1836"]*, and was interested in it.

January 11: Beautiful soft day, with clear sunshine; quite like spring; wrote a sermon on the calling of the Gentiles. Nothing particular occurred.

January 12 (Sunday): Very pleasing day upon the whole; services all right and music excellent. Chapel very well filled considering the season.

January 13: Weather fair and mild; thermometer at 45°*[F; 7°C]*.

January 14: Read a very clever kind of novel: "The Widow Barnaby" by Mrs. Trollope *[Frances Milton Trollope, 1780–1863]*; plasterwork behind the altar begun.

January 15: Weather continues beautiful; letter from Mr Walker of Huntly; much occupied and variously; Sarah succeeding very well in her organ playing; work xxxxxx *[?remiss]*.

January 16: Cold, blustering day with showers; went to Moy-hall to call for Mackintosh (Johnny with me); returned home at 4 o'clock wet and cold; found a note to Mrs F. from Lady Saltoun asking us to dine at Ness Castle tomorrow.

January 17: Part of forenoon in the Chapel; dined at Lady Saltoun's, where I met Sir F. and Lady Mackenzie. Mrs Fyvie met me at Ness Cottage on returning, and we walked home rather late, but beautiful evening.

January 18: Nothing particular; wrote a letter to Bp. Low; prepared as usual for Sunday.

January 19 (Sunday): An uncommonly bad day – wind and rain, quite tempestuous – congregation thin, services well-performed and music magnificently fine. Did not preach in the afternoon (dined by daylight for 1st time).

January 20: Wind and rain; very stormy.

January 21: Ditto, ditto. Nothing particular occurred.

January 22: Rather much the same; wrote several letters.

January 23: Day mild and rainy; nothing particular occurred.

January 24: An awful storm of wind and sleet from the N.W.; did great damage to houses in the neighbourhood; continued throughout the whole day and night.

January 25: Still stormy; occupied much as usual during the day. At about eleven o'clock at night was suddenly called upon to cross over into Ross-shire to baptise an infant (Capt. and Mrs Fraser's cottage), supposed dying; passed the Ferry at Kessock a little after 12, walked on to Capt. Fraser's and baptised the infant who was very weak; returned home a little before 4 in the morning much fatigued.

January 26 (Sunday): A miserably bad day and the Chapel very thin – nobody almost from the landward – dined at Mr G. Anderson's.

January 27: Very stormy; buried the infant I had baptised on Saturday; nothing further occurred worthy of notice.

January 28: Steady clear winter day; in town in the forenoon; wrote several letters, one to Sir G. Prevost in reply to his of Saturday.

January 29: Frost and sunshine, with about 3 inches of snow.

January 30: Do., do., nothing particular occurred; wrote to Miss Prevost, and spent part of the forenoon in new Chapel. Morning and evening engaged in teaching the boys as usual every day. Heard of Mrs Macfarlane's arrival from India.

January 31: A fine mild day; had door broken through the eastern gable of the Chapel for a new access to the vestry.

February 1: Occupied as usual on Saturdays, nothing particular.

February 2 (Sunday): A good deal of snow and very cold, Chapel pretty full notwithstanding, and both services quite satisfactory – chanting excellent.

February 3: Nothing particular occurred, weather mild.

February 4: Do., do., do., do.

February 5: Stormy weather and high winds, but not very cold.

February 6: Fast before the Sacrament at the Kirk; Eliza and Matilda Fraser called; wrote several letters, nothing particular.

February 7: Dined at Ness Cottage, walked home by the town, the night exceedingly rough and boisterous with very heavy showers. Sarah makes great progress.

February 8: Cold stormy day; work about the altar finished; employed much as usual. Mrs Macfarlane arrived at Kingsmills from India.

February 9 (Sunday): Heavy snow and some drift, Chapel rather thin in consequence; nothing particular in the services – music exceedingly good. Mrs F. walked home by Kingsmills and saw Mrs Macfarlane.

February 10: The Queen's marriage day; fine mild weather.

February 11: Walked with Johnny to the Hon. Mr Fraser's at Laggan Cottage; engaged to send him there 3 times a week to give lessons to one of the boys.

February 12: Fine spring-looking day; nothing particular.

February 13: Dined at Muirtown with Mrs. F.; walked home very early; fireworks in the town on account of the Queen's marriage *[to Albert]*.

February 14: Went to Cromarty with Maggy on her way to London by sea *[to attend school, aged 18]*; the weather uncommonly fine. Mrs F. and I returned very late or rather early.

February 15: Busy all the forenoon about various things; dined at Muirtown with Mrs F.; returned home at 8 o'clock; reading last 2 numbers of the quarterly "Theological Review" *[probably: The British Critic, Quarterly Theological Review, and Ecclesiastical Record]*.

February 16 (Sunday): A very wet day, and chapel rather thinly attended; baptised Mr G. Anderson's infant between services.

February 17: A beautiful day, received several letters and made a number of professional calls; reading "British Critic".

February 18: Much the same as yesterday every way.

February 19: Nothing particular occurred.

February 20: Ditto,   do.,   weather calm and rather mild.

February 21: Occupied much as usual.

February 22: We were much disappointed to find by a letter from Maggy that the London *[vessel]* had not left Cromarty Bay in consequence of the prevailing easterly winds; practising, etc., as usual.

February 23 (Sunday): Preached on "The Sepulchre in the Garden"; Chapel very well attended; Mrs Macfarlane there for the first time since her return from India. Mrs F. went to Muirtown after morning church, to enquire for Mrs Warrand's little boy who is dangerously ill of an attack of inflammation.

February 24: Dry, cold and frosty; called at Muirtown to enquire for Mrs W.'s little boy still very ill. Maggy returned from Cromarty after being for 10 days on board ship in the bay. Heard about <u>new organ</u> and of a burgh election immediately to take place.

February 25: Frosty and clear, roads drifting with dust. Mrs F. went to Muirtown while I made various calls, and engaged a berth for Maggy on board the "North Star" steamer to sail on Monday first. *[The "North Star" sailed from Thornbush Quay to London on alternate Mondays].*

February 26: Nothing particular to report; cold frosty weather and no snow.

February 27: Mr Mackintosh, Daviot, Miss J. McIntosh and the Miss Frasers, Ness Cottage, dined with us.

February 28: Day of nomination for the approaching ~~Burgh~~ *[sic]* election of an MP for the Burghs. Mr John Fraser *[Cromarty House, a native of Inverness]*, the Conservative, and Mr Morrison (London), the radical *[Whig]* candidate; did not go near the hustings. A miserably cold day.

[From 1708 until 1918 the Inverness Burghs constituency consisted of Inverness, Fortrose, Forres and Nairn. In early 1840, Mr Roderick Macleod of Cadboll (1786–1853), the sitting Whig MP for the Inverness Burghs, was in declining health, and stood down without waiting for a General Election. Mr James Morrison, London merchant/millionaire, contested the seat in his place for the Whigs/Liberals. Earlier in February he had been in Inverness for some days accompanied by Mr Edward Ellis, MP, but had left before the writ for the election was issued. He promptly returned. The contest on 3rd March was won by Morrison by 353 votes to 308. Morrison had previously been MP for St. Ives (1830–1832) and Ipswich (1831–1835). He was returned unopposed in the General Election of 1841, and continued as the Inverness Burghs MP until 1847, when he retired through failing health. A separate MP was elected for the County of Inverness.]

February 29: Clear and pleasant day; employed much as usual on Saturdays; town in great bustle.

March 1 (Sunday): Chapel very fairly attended; in the afternoon particularly hard frost, without snow.

March 2: A fine day, cold and sharp, but clear; saw Maggy on the steamer for London at 8 p.m., sailed at 10.

March 3: The election is over. 41 of a majority *[press reports say 45 – see above]* in favour of the Whig-Radical member.
> Oh, I loe weel my Charlie's name.
> Tho' some there be that abhor him,
> But, Oh! to see the De'el gang hame
> Wi' a' the Whigs before him.
>   Over the water etc. etc.
>   (*Vide* "Red Gauntlet", vol. 2)

What a contrast between the miserable rabble of would-be Highlanders who disgraced our streets to-day with the Highlanders of other days!!

March 4 (Ash Wednesday): After Church Service Mrs. F. and I and the children walked to Muirtown. The declaration from the hustings was <u>performed</u>. Mr Fraser did not appear – a very wise step. Conservative party met in the larger room in the Caledonian Hotel.

March 5: Nothing particular occurred – clear and frosty.

March 6: Ditto,   ditto.

March 7: As usual on Saturdays; day very mild and warm.

March 8 (Sunday): The day uncommonly fine, but from various causes (from colds, etc.) Chapel rather thinner than usual; nothing particular occurred.

March 9: Engaged about the Chapel; called at Raigmore's, and Capt. D. Mackintosh's, etc., etc.

March 10: Reading Sir W. Scott's "Life of Napoleon" *[1820's]*. A most beautiful day. Mrs F. and I walked home by Ness Cottage; heard from Maggy of her safe arrival in London.

March 11: Received a notification of the death of Bishop *[George]* Gleig (on the 9th Inst.) *[1753–1840, Bishop of Brechin from 1810 and Primus from 1816]* – he had outlived all his mental faculties. Made several professional calls, after prayers in the Chapel, and returned from town early.

March 12: Received the melancholy intelligence of the death of the Master of Grant *[Francis William Grant, who died "from an affection of the heart", aged 26]*, MP for the County *[elected at 1838 by-election, Conservative]* – he was found dead in bed on the morning of the 11th at Cullen House, where he had arrived the previous night from London to make arrangements for the funeral of his mother, the Hon. Mrs Grant of Grant. "Lord, what is man and what is his life" *[based on Jeremiah x.23]*.

March 13: A vexatious kind of day altogether.

March 14: Wrote a sermon on "Be sure your sin will find you out" *[Numbers xxxii.23]*. A beautiful, mild, soft day, and towards evening some beautiful showers.

March 15 (Sunday): Rained rather heavily in the morning, which prevented many from going to church – sermon seemed to attract peculiar attention. G. Anderson dined with us in the evening – had a good deal of very interesting conversation. The sweetest day that I remember at this season – rather like May than March.

March 16: Reading W. Scott's "Life of Napoleon".

March 17: Nothing particular occurred.

March 18: Beautiful day. New organ arrived – saw it safely from board ship and stowed inside the Chapel. Finished 3rd volume of "Napoleon".

March 19: Walked to Hon. Mr Fraser's and back to Mrs Fraser (Ness Cottage) to dinner. Mrs F. came to tea, and we walked home by the town, evening being beautiful. Whig party retired from contesting the county, and Mr Henry Baillie *[of Tarradale – Conservative]* to be returned without opposition in room of the late Master of Grant. *[A few days later Henry Baillie was nominated by Cluny Macpherson, and seconded by Mr Macallister, Tallisker, Skye.]*

March 20: Nothing occurred worthy of notice; weather dry and cold.

March 21: Occupied as usual on Saturdays.

March 22 (Sunday): Church pretty full both forenoon and afternoon; had a letter from Maggy, giving account of how she is occupied at school, etc. Weather fine but rather cold.

March 23: Very cold with easterly wind; read the first 2 vols. of "The Doctor", a very singular talented work, anonymously written. *[Probably the book by Robert Southey (1774–1843), first published anonymously in 1834.]*

March 24: Nothing occurred worthy of remark in these memoranda.

March 25: Cold and dry; farmers busy sowing. After prayers in Chapel made some calls; saw Matilda and Alex Fraser with the "Star" Coach on their way to Dalvey.

March 26: Weather mild; still reading "The Doctor".

March 27: Finished "The Doctor". Had the partition between our bedroom and the study taken away. In reading "The Doctor" was struck with the following passage with reference to will-making:

> They who think that in the testamentary disposal of their property they have the right to do whatever it is legally in their power to do, may find themselves woefully mistaken when they come to render their account. Nothing but the weightiest moral considerations can justify anyone in

depriving another of that which the law of the land would otherwise in its due course have assigned him.

Garden operations far advanced – sowed carrot, turnip, lettuce, etc. (a + day however), vexed spirit.

March 28: A beautiful day, engaged much as usual on Saturdays; nothing particular occurred.

March 29 *[Sunday]*: Very exhilarating day every way almost – soft and warm as May. Chapel very well attended indeed, and both services very satisfactory – sermons I hope did good – heard of Maggie by a letter from Mr Bowdler to Mrs. F. Began to prepare sermon for opening *[of]* new organ on Saturday 11th April.

March 30: Weather somewhat cold; nothing particular.

March 31: Ditto.

April 1: Prayers in Chapel as usual. Mr *[James]* Bruce *[Edinburgh organ-builder, active 1803–1849]* arrived to put up the new organ.

April 2: Occupied most of the day in taking down old organ; day cold and showery.

April 3: Advancing with new organ, and got some additional subscriptions.

April 4: Sold old organ and had it removed; new one partly put together and looking <u>magnificent</u>.

April 5 (Sunday): A pleasing day; Chapel well attended and singing good with no organ accompaniment. Mr Bruce dined with us. Weather mild and pleasant.

April 6: Very much occupied about putting up the new organ; weather cold and showery filling up the *[sentence stops here]*

April 7, 8, 9, 10: Just as above in every respect.

April 11: New organ publicly opened. <u>Noble instrument</u>. A wet day and many prevented from attending. *[Special service included a performance of Kent's "Hear my Prayer" – see May 21, 1839 and "Inverness Courier" report of the service.]* Collection £12. Heard of the death of Mrs Mackintosh of Mackintosh in London on Tuesday the 7th.

April 12 (Sunday): Chapel well attended. <u>Music quite rapturous</u>, Service very impressive, and I trust edifying to all.

April 13: Nothing particular occurred.

April 14: An uncommonly hot day; Mrs F. not very well and had some difficulty in getting home from town.

April 15: Weather quite warm; went in the evening to Kessock Ferry to meet the remains of Mrs Mackintosh of Mackintosh which were conveyed by steam*[er]* from London.

April 16: Very beautiful day; daily services as usual during the holy week. Nothing particular occurred.

April 17 (Good Friday): Chapel rather thinly attended from various causes. Weather perfectly beautiful; returned home early. A good deal of varied incident during the day, but nothing remarkable. The new organ a great source of elevating pleasure to me. Mem.: The metrical psalms selected for the day seemed very applicable, viz.– last 3 v. of the 23rd, and the 2nd part of my selection from the 66th, the first to *[the tune]* Martyrdom, the 2nd to Orton *[this may be a reference to the setting in a book of psalms and hymns published by Job Orton in 1755]*.

April 18: Prayers in Chapel; practice of music for Easter. Drove to Daviot to call for Mr En*[eas]* M*[ackintosh]* and Mrs Troughton, and returned home before dinner.

April 19 (Easter Day): The fullest congregation I ever saw in Inverness – the service quite exhilarating throughout. Music admirable, sermon listened to with great attention and I trust with profit to many. In consequence of the absence of several *[of]* our principal members, especially the whole Mackintosh family and relatives, the number of communicants was less than might be expected, the number being about 70. A lovely day as to weather, although a little easterly wind.

April 20: After morning prayers, made several calls in town and then went to Moy Hall to see Mackintosh after his arrival from London; staid *[sic]* for dinner and returned home in the evening.

April 21: The assizes – went into the Court for a little with Johnny; met Mr Dunbar of Northfield, and saw several acquaintances from Ross and Moray shires.

April 22: Dined at Raigmore's with Mrs F. to meet Mr Dunbar; a beautiful day.

April 23: Mr Dunbar came early to arrange with Miss Banyon as governess to his children – they were mutually pleased with each other and the arrangement promises well. This day was held as a fast (i.e., a surfeit of preaching) in the Kirk, on account of the troubles of which the Presbyterian Ministers themselves were the originators, and in which they continue the agitators!!

April 24: Funeral of Mrs Mackintosh of Mackintosh. Went to Moy Hall early – burial service in part there and partly at Petty. A most beautiful day – returned from the funeral about 4 o'clock. Mrs F. and I walked to Ness Cottage in the evening; never saw such weather at this season.

April 25: Nothing very particular; various little crosses, not the less trying because private. Saw poor Jane Hunter (Mrs Sewell) again for the first time since her marriage on this day in 1838. Preparations for Sunday as usual.

April 26 (Sunday): Church well attended, sermons on St. Thomas' unbelief; listened to with great attention; music quite excellent.

April 27: A lovely day – we all crossed the ferry and Mrs F. and I called at Craigton Cottage on Capt. and Mrs Fraser, while the boys went on to Kilmuir; on our way home drank tea at Muirtown – a most enjoyable day.

April 28: Mrs Sewel and Eliza Hunter dined with us; E. and M. Fraser came to tea – a most beautiful day.

April 29: Nothing particular occurred – perfectly summer weather.

April 30: Attended Mr Mackintosh's lectures on geology in the Academy Hall. *[Details about the lecturer could not be identified.]*

May 1: A lovely day – nothing particular occurred.

May 2: Employed as usual on Saturdays.

May 3 (Sunday): Day quite hot. Chapel very well attended. Mr and Mrs Pearson and children dined with us.

May 4: Misty with some fine small rain towards the afternoon; attended the 3rd geological lecture.

May 5: Had rained heavily all night, continued to do so most of the day; dined at Kingsmills. Dr Munro arrived late at night after an absence of about 13 months.

May 6: Dry again, but much cooler; saw Dr Munro and very glad to see him look so well; nothing particular occurred.

May 7: A coldish day. Mrs *[F.]* and I dined at Muirtown, rained very heavily in the evening; on our way home called for Mr and Mrs Pearson and took them up to sleep at Roseheath.

May 8: Took Dr Munro to see the Chapel; day wet and cold.

May 9: Weather very cold with snow on the heights.

May 10 (Sunday): A very cold unpleasant day and Chapel consequently thinly attended; services satisfactory however, and I hope profitable to many.

May 11: Weather cold and rainy; nothing particular.

May 12: Ditto;   heard of the murder of Lord W*[illiam]* Russell *[a former Whig MP, murdered by his valet]*.

May 13: Ditto,   ditto.

May 14: A beautiful day, mild and sunny. Matilda dined with us; Mrs F. and I went with her to Mr Mackintosh's evening lecture in the Infant School, and afterwards to Ness Cottage; returned home about half past 11; evening quite beautiful.

May 15: Day somewhat cold and wet with wind from the east.

May 16: Rained heavily the whole day, but not cold; nothing particular occurred.

May 17 *[Sunday]*: Snow lying on the adjoining heights as near to us as Inshes and along the Leys; pouring rain with us and very cold. Chapel uncommonly ill attended in consequence. Received an interesting communication from Mr Ogleby about an Episcopal Chapel in the vale of Urquhart *[presumably leading to St. Ninian's, Glenurquhart, in 1884]*. On our way home from Church, called to see baby Munro, this being her birth day; scarcely ever remember such a day at this season.

May 18: Weather just as yesterday; dined at Dr Munro's. Mrs F. and I walked home late.

May 19: Day a shade milder, but snow still lying deep on the heights; nothing occurred worthy of notice.

May 20: Transacted a good deal of business. Dr and Mrs Munro came to hear the organ; spent some time with them in the Chapel.

May 21: Wind still easterly and cold, but dry; walked to Clachnaharry with Dr and Mrs Munro and a few others to look at geological phenomena. Mrs F. confined with a cold.

May 22: Wind changed to southwest, mild and genial; wrote and dispatched several letters.

May 23: First observed pease in blossom in the garden; day spent as usual on Saturdays.

May 24 (Sunday): Mrs *[F.]* confined by a severe cold; day not very favourable but Church pretty full, and both services very satisfactory. Dined with Mr G. Anderson.

May 25: Kept as the Queen's birthday.

May 26: Weather much milder, but with high wind; in the evening called at Heath Cottage for Mrs Macpherson, whose house had been broken into on Sunday morning.

May 27: Nothing particular occurred.

May 28 (Ascension): Prayers in Chapel, indifferently attended. A beautiful day, with rather high wind.

May 29: Received a letter from Wick about opening Episcopal Chapel there *[church established there from 1867]*; nothing particular occurred.

May 30: Employed as usual on Saturdays; nothing particular. Weather windy and showery.

May 31 (Sunday): A fine day and a good congregation; preached twice on the subject of the Ascension. Mr G. Mackenzie's boys dined with us. The day altogether has left a very pleasing impression. I hope has been edifying.

June 1: Had a letter from Sir G. Mackenzie inviting us to Coul.

June 2: In town most of the day, and called at Ness Cottage in the evening. Mrs F.'s cold still continues, although improved.

June 3: Dined at Mr G. Anderson's with the Miss Patersons.

June 4: Read Miss Sinclair's new vol. "Shetland and the Shetlanders" *[Catherine Sinclair, 1800–1864, book published 1840]*; nothing particular occurred.

June 5: Mr Warrand dined with us. Dr Munro, Mrs Schrouxxxxx and the Miss Frasers, Ness Cottage, to tea.

June 6: Occupied as usual on Saturdays.

June 7 (Whitsunday): A fine day and rather full church (50

communicants); the services very satisfactory and beautifully impressive, music capital.

June 8: Prayers in church tolerably well attended; made several calls afterwards.

June 9: Mrs F. and I went to Coul; rained most of the day; arrived at Coul at 6 in time to dinner.

June 10: Drove out to see Loch Achilty and the falls of the Conan, and afterwards walked about the beautiful garden and grounds until 6 o'clock. In the evening had some sacred music on the organ by our organist, Mr Jackson *[had been a pupil of Dr. Matthew Camidge, York Minster]*.

June 11: Got up early and reached Kessock in Sir George's carriage by 9 o'clock; married Mary Paterson at eleven; came home to Roseheath, returned to town to dine with a few of the marriage party, and walked about the town in the evening with Rev. Mr *[James Spencer]* Knox, Vicar General of Derry, who was introduced by Bp. Walker and Mr Ramsay; a very intelligent pleasant man, whom I shall be glad to meet again. *[Knox died in 1862 aged 72.]*

June 12: Mrs F. and I dined at Kingsmills; received an excellent letter from Mackintosh of Mackintosh, expressed with great good feeling and enclosing 20 pounds for the organ.

June 13: As usual on Saturdays, nothing particular occurred. Mrs F. and I drank tea at Dr Munro's and staid *[sic]* rather late; reading the preface to the new edition of Knox's liturgy. *[William Knox, 1732–1810, "Observations upon the Liturgy".]*

June 14 (Trinity Sunday): Preached twice upon appropriate subjects for the day. Chapel very well filled; observed some tourists for the first time this season. Dr Munro dropt in to tea, and we had a deal of interesting conversation.

June 15: An uncomfortable day altogether, but beautiful weather and the face of the earth lovely.

June 16: Dark, wet and very windy.

June 17: Showery, and wind; very boisterous; after attending the Infirmary committee called at Ness Cottage for Eliza. Mrs Fraser, Matilda and Aleck at Burghead. Great excitement about the murderous attempt on the life of the Queen. *[The first of several attempts to assassinate Queen Victoria, this one by Edward Oxford, while she was riding in a carriage with Prince Albert to visit her mother; two bullets were fired but both missed; Oxford was tried for high treason, and found guilty, but was acquitted on grounds of insanity.]*

June 18: Weather much the same in every respect; nothing particular occurred; reading Croly's "Life of Burke" *[George Croly, 1780–1860: "A Memoir of the Political Life of the Right Honourable Edmund Burke; with extracts from his writing" (1840)]*; had a letter from Mr Maclauren proposing an exchange of duty for Sunday week (2 Trinity).

June 19: Showery and cold; nothing particular occurred.

June 20: Ditto,   ditto.

June 21 (Sunday *[1 Trinity]*): Pouring rain in torrents and congregation thin in consequence; dined at Dr Munro's.

June 22: The heaviest rain I remember, and all day.

June 23: Cold and showery; nothing particular occurred.

June 24: Attended committee at the Infirmary; afterwards to the flower show in the Northern Meeting Rooms.

June 25: Fast Thursday as they call it in <u>the Kirk</u>; weather clear again and quite warm towards evening. Miss Prevost arrived in the afternoon and Mrs F. and I went in the evening to see her.

June 26: Started by the "Defiance" at 6 in the morning for Elgin, arrived there at eleven, made several calls and baptised Mr Maclauren's baby (Helen); spent the rest of the day with Mr Maclauren very agreeably and had a great variety of conversation. Mem.: Try to remember the story of the Highlander when he heard High Mass in St. Peter's: "Och! she never saw, etc., etc., treated like a shentleman before" and the Irishwoman following her son to the gallows, crying "Oh, Pat, I hope you'll take warning by the example."

June 27: Breakfasted at Sir A. Dunbar's and then walked to Duffus; called at Duffus House, and dined with Mrs Adam *[presumably the mother of Dean Fyvie's first wife]* afterwards; walked into Elgin in the evening and slept as on the previous night at Mr Mark's at the Grey Friars; rained most of the day.

June 28 (Sunday, 2 Trinity): Officiated in Trinity Chapel, Elgin, Mr Maclauren taking the duty at Inverness (Sarah played the organ for the first time on a Sunday); an attentive congregation and a most beautiful day. Dined at *[sic]* passed the evening at Sir A. Dunbar's.

June 29: Returned to Inverness by the "Star" coach and found all

70

well (D.G.), Mr Maclauren, Miss Prevost and Dr Munro dined at Roseheath; floods of talk after tea (had new potatoes from our own garden for first time).

June 30: Most of the forenoon in the Chapel with Mr Maclauren to hear some sacred music by Jackson *[the organist]*; drank tea and staid late at Dr Munro, having had a deal of exciting conversation.

July 1: A quieter day.

July 2: Mr Maclauren left early in the morning, with a lovely day; nothing particular occurred. Johnny and I dined at Miss Prevost's, Mrs F. not being very well.; walked down to tea. Received several letters, some of them rather perplexing (+ day)

July 3: A drizzly day; Mrs F. and I took a gig to Nairn and engaged a lodging for her for sea bathing.

July 4: Still showery but warmer, made new arrangement with Jackson; Matilda and Aleck Fraser to tea at Roseheath after their return from Burghead; walked down with them in the rain to top of Castle Street, as they were to call on Miss Prevost on their way home.

July 5 (Sunday, 3 Trinity): Heavy rain all the forenoon; officiated at Inverness forenoon and afternoon, and at Fort George to the Royal Regiment at half past 5, and reached home at 9 fagged, but scarcely so very much as on former occasions; services all satisfactory; Chapel not very full from the heavy rain.

July 6: A beautiful day; Mrs F. and Jamie went to Nairn for sea bathing; dined at Miss Prevost's with Matilda and Aleck Fraser, and walked home with them to Ness Cottage in the evening.

July 7: Warm and showery; dined at Muirtown with Johnny and Charlie; heard from Mrs. F. – all well at Nairn.

July 8: Warm and showery still; at home all day except an hour in town; went to the steam boat expecting Mr Macgregor from Fort William, but he has not made his appearance. Wool fair tomorrow.

July 9: Very rainy all day; got up at 4 o'clock and went with Johnny to the steam boat on his way to Polmaly *[near Drumnadrochit]*. Mr Macgregor and his little boy arrived.

July 10: Very heavy rain. Mrs F. returned from Nairn per "Star" *[coach]*. I dined at Dr Munro's; Mrs F. with Miss Prevost; returned home together at 9; much conversation with Mr Macgregor.

July 11: Continued rain with easterly wind.

July 12 (Sunday, 4 Trinity): Rain all the day. Chapel very full in consequence of the general influx of strangers attending the Wool Fair. Officiated at Fort George at half past 5; dined afterwards with the officers of the Royal Regiment and returned home between 10 and 11; a fatiguing but pleasant day.

July 13: Day cleared up; Mrs *[F.]* and I went in a gig to Moy leaving Charlie at Nairn on our way down.

July 14: After a most delightful evening and forenoon spent with the Miss Cumming's *[sic]*, returned to Inverness in the evening leaving Mrs F. at Nairn to pursue her sea bathing which is of great benefit to her.

July 15: Almost incessant rain; wrote some letters and towards afternoon wrought a little in the garden. Mrs Macpherson, Heath Cottage, called in the evening.

July 16: Day damp with some heavy showers; dined at Muirtown and met the Mackenzies of Mount Gerald *[a nineteenth-century mansion two miles north of Dingwall, and originally called Clyne]*.

July 17 *[date incorrectly given as 16]*: Day the same – dined again at Muirtown.

July 18 *[date incorrectly given as 17]*: Mrs Fyvie returned from Nairn per "Star" coach; day mild and had a quiet evening to prepare for Sunday.

July 19 (Sunday, 5 Trinity): A very full church both in the forenoon and afternoon. I trust some good doing. To Fort George in the evening as usual, and returned about 10; all well, but much fatigued. Showery day.

July 20: Wet day; attended examination of the Greek, Latin and French classes in the *[Royal]* Academy.

July 21: Attended examination of the Mathematical class, and greatly pleased. Orations *[end-of-session public recitations, poems, etc., performed by pupils]* afterwards, Miss Prevost there. Mrs Simpson and her daughters dined with us; M. and A. Fraser to tea; walked home with them at night. Mrs S. and daughters staying all night; rather rainy.

July 22: Weather still wet; Mrs S. and daughters dined with us again; nothing particular occurred.

July 23: A fine day, dry throughout but little sunshine. Miss Prevost, Miss Frasers, Mr and Mrs G. Anderson, Mrs A. Mackenzie, etc., to tea.

July 24: Visit to Cawdor Castle with Miss Prevost – a beautiful and very enjoyable day. Mrs F. bathed at Nairn; returned home about 10. Eliza and Aleck Fraser of our party – a sort of sunbeam day.

July 25: A beautiful day; Miss Prevost dined with us.

July 26 (Sunday, 6 Trinity): A fine day and a full church (Mrs Maclachlan there). Services very satisfactory throughout; at Fort George the same. Rev. Mr Samson read prayers there and I preached; returned safely to Roseheath about 10 o'clock.

July 27: Went to Strathpeffer with Miss Prevost, Mrs F. and Eliza Fraser (Mem.: Salome); reached Inverness at 9 and took tea with Miss Prevost – a fine day with one heavy shower.

July 28: Nothing particular occurred; walked to Ness Cottage in the evening and sat there a little – a beautiful night and enjoyed the walk home.

July 29: Attended Infirmary committee and made various professional calls.

July 30: Wind and showers; baptised Mr C. Gordon's child in Church; afterwards called at Kingsmills and saw Mr Maclachlan. Johnny at Struy with Miss Prevost and M. Fraser. Wrote several letters and afterwards in the garden.

July 31: Dined (with Mrs F.) at Ness Cottage expecting the return of the party from Struy. They did not arrive until 7 o'clock in consequence of an accident occurring on the way.

August 1: A fine day. Johnny and I dined at Muirtown, and waited the arrival of the steamboat, expecting Miss Shadwell and friend – did not arrive till late, and we returned home before.

August 2 (Sunday, 7 Trinity): A beautiful day and a full Church; everything satisfactory throughout; the Dunmaglasse's *[sic]* for the first time since their arrival *[Dunmaglass was the historic seat of the Clan MacGillivray]*; returned from Fort George in time to tea at Dr Munro's.

August 3: Had a large party to dinner to meet Miss Prevost. A beautiful night, walked part of the way home with Matilda and Alexr. Fraser.

August 4: A very fine day; saw Miss Prevost and Alexr. F. off to Strathpeffer; afterwards we dined at Kingsmills. A pleasant day and weather delightful.

August 5: Dined at Kingsmills.

August 6: Dined at Muirtown with Miss Shadwell, Mr Maclachlan, etc., etc. Mrs F. and I came home in a phaeton *[an open carriage drawn by a single horse]*.

August 7: Very hot day. Mrs Macfarlane and Mrs Maclachlan dined at Roseheath; made several calls in the forenoon.

August 8: <u>Excessively hot</u>; home all day, wrote several letters, etc., etc. Prepared sermon for Sunday.

August 9 (Sunday, 8 Trinity): What a day? Mr Lapremandaye, Mr Povah, Mr Troughton – gloriously Catholic – quite a field day. To the Fort in the evening and back to tea at Dr Munro's.

August 10: To Strathpeffer with Mr and Mrs Lapremandaye, etc., etc.; dined with Miss Prevost there, and returned very late.

August 11: Passed the whole day at home with our new acquaintances. E. and M. Fraser of the party in the afternoon; dancing by Mrs L. and P.

August 12: To the Fall of Foyers with Mr and Mrs L. and Mr P. – a <u>delightfully</u> delightful day, ever to be remembered with satisfaction, and not to be forgotten; back to Ness Cottage to tea.

August 13: Agreeably surprised by the arrival of Mr Majendie *[possibly Major John Routledge Majendie, 1801–1850]*; had a small party to meet him, and all passed most beautifully; went over the new Chapel with Mr Majendie in the forenoon, organ, etc. Anecdote of an hostler *[stableman for horses]* at York about Church service <u>starting</u> exactly at quarter before eleven: "They starts Sir precisely at quarter before 11".

August 14: A busy day, but nothing particular; dined at Drummond.

August 15: Prayers in Chapel at 11 – as usual on Saturdays.

August 16 (Sunday, 9 Trinity): Sixty communicants, I hope a gracious day. Mr Troughton read prayers forenoon and afternoon; a well-filled Chapel. Dr Munro went with me to Fort George, and came home with me and had some supper and some good conversation.

August 17: A regular storm of wind and rain the whole day. Mrs F.

and I dined at Muirtown to meet Mrs and Miss Dick; in the forenoon had a meeting of the building committee in the vestry.

August 18: Soft and a little showery; called at Lady Saltoun's and at Ness Cottage; afterwards dined at Raigmore's to meet a Mr and Mrs Bridgeman Simpson [possibly the former MP for Wenlock and his wife].

August 19: A beautiful day; walked round the Longman with Dr Munro; wrote some letters, etc., etc. Mrs Warrand, Mrs Dick and her daughter, Miss Mackintosh and Miss Hilier dined at Roseheath.

August 20: Nothing particular occurred.

August 21: Very warm day; dined at Daviot and called at Leys Castle on the Whites, on our way.

August 22: Extremely hot; engaged in the Chapel all the forenoon, and afterwards dined at Ness Cottage to meet Capt. Greenwood; came home early.

August 23 (Sunday, 10 Trinity): Upon the whole a very spirit-stirring day; fine and very attentive congregation. After the [services] were over here, Mr Troughton and Mr Æneas Mackintosh went with me to the Fort where Mr Troughton read prayers and preached; returned to Roseheath where we joined Mrs Troughton. The weather beautiful and very warm.

August 24: A lovely day; nothing particular occurred.

August 25: Baptised Mr Peter Anderson's child, and dined there afterwards. Mr [John] Murdoch [incumbent, Keith, 1800–1850], Mr Maclauren and Mr Douphrate [incumbent, Fochabers, 1840–1847] arrived in the evening.

August 26: The Synod of the Clergy of Moray and Ross met at 11. Mr Troughton read prayers. The clerical business passed off pleasantly. All the clergy dined with us and a pretty large party – Miss Prevost, etc., etc.

August 27: A very warm day. Walked with Mrs Douphrate, Mr Maclauren and Dr Munro all the forenoon; called at Muirtown and after dining at home we all went to tea at Ness Cottage.

August 28: Still warm; walked as far as Culloden Muir with Dr Munro to convey Messrs Maclauren and Douphrate on their way homeward. Mrs F. and I afterwards dined at Lady Saltoun's and met Lord Saltoun, Lord Selkirk, etc. – a <u>worthless</u> evening, although beautiful in itself.

August 29: Warm and beautiful; harvest fairly begun with beautiful crops (D.G.); employed as usual on Saturdays.

August 30 (Sunday): A beautiful day and a very full Church. Mr Troughton read prayers both forenoon and afternoon; got home from the Fort in very good time – a very animating day altogether.

August 31: Day warm and beautiful; dined at Raigmore's and met the Tytlers; at home all the forenoon writing letters, etc., etc.

September 1: Very warm and sultry; nothing particular occurred.

September 2: Rain in the latter part of the day. Mr Murdoch arrived on his way back from Fort William.

September 3: Weather soft and fine; Mr Murdoch left by the "Star" coach on his way home. Johnny went to Polmaly by the boat at 5 in the morning. Walked to Ness Cottage in the evening having heard of John [Fraser]'s expected arrival by the London steamer tomorrow.

September 4: In town early; variously occupied in the forenoon (pulling pears, apples, etc., with Jamie in the garden behind the Chapel); afterwards Mrs F. joined – Charlie and Sarah. "North Star" steamer arrived at 9 o'clock but could not land passengers till day light.

September 5: A most beautiful day; walked to Ness Cottage early and saw John Fraser – went afterwards with him, Eliza and Aleck to town, and spent some time in the Chapel with them; went home early to make arrangements for Sunday.

September 6 (Sunday, 12 Trinity): A fine day, and well-filled Church; to Fort George as usual; returned to tea at Dr Munro's. Mr Troughton read prayers at Inverness forenoon and afternoon.

September 7: Nothing particular occurred.

September 8: Rained part of the day. Mrs John Anderson and her boys dined with us.

September 9: Fine day but very windy. We dined at Ness Cottage.

September 10: Weather squally with occasional showers. Went early to town to meet Miss Erskin from Coul; in waiting for her, met in with Rev. Mr Mostyn of Greenock [incumbent, 1840–1844]. Walked to the islands with Miss Erskin; told me some amusing anecdotes about the ignorance of children taught in Presbyterian schools – one was about a girl who on being asked who <u>Adam</u> was, answered – <u>"Eve"</u>. After dinner saw her on board the steamer in Kessock ferry – the night becoming excessively stormy, had some difficulty in getting on shore and did not get home till nearly eleven o'clock, quite wet; and Mrs F. alarmed and afraid of some accident having happened.

September 11: Weather squally, and sometimes boisterous; baptised Mr Rennie's child; nothing particular occurred.

September 12: John Fraser, his sisters, Matilda and Aleck, Mrs Troughton, Mr Troughton, Mr En. Mackintosh, Mr Mostyn, etc., dined with us. Johnny returned from Polmaly.

September 13 (Sunday, 13 Trinity): Mr Mostyn read prayers and preached in the morning; Mr Troughton and I taking the Altar service; in the evening Mr Troughton lead prayers and Mr Mostyn preached. Set off for Fort G. before the sermon in the evening. N.B. Mr Mostyn and J. Strachan's watch!!

September 14: Spent the day at home, and worked a good deal in the garden with the boys in the forenoon; easterly wind with sunshine, and snow on Wyvis for the first time in the season, but fine harvest day.

September 15: At home all the forenoon; sunshine, but cold; rather severe frost during the night and potatoes quite blackened.

September 16: Rain with easterly wind, very disagreeable; walked from the Infirmary with Dr Munro by the islands to Ness Cottage for a call. In the evening I dined at Mr G. Anderson's to meet John Fraser, etc., etc., the Miss Stuarts from Stirling being at Roseheath with Mrs F.

September 17: Storm abated but wind still easterly.

September 18: Much and variously occupied all day. Mr Dalton [evangelic Anglican clergyman from Ulster, at that point minister of St. Paul's, Wolverhampton] arrived, Mr Fraser, Struy, etc., etc.; visited some sick persons; day cold and raw.

September 19: Mr Dalton kindly offered to preach twice on Sunday, so was relieved of part of this day's labour. Mr and Mrs Dalton, Mr Hugh Fraser, and John, Matilda and the two Miss Stuarts dined with us. Miss Prevost came from Strathpeffer in time to tea.

September 20 (Sunday, 14 Trinity): Altogether a blessed day – a splendid congregation and two capital sermons from Mr Dalton. I read prayers in the morning and Mr Troughton in the evening. Fort George as usual; back to tea with Miss Prevost and joined Mrs F.; called afterwards at the Union Hotel for Mr Dalton, and were present at prayers there with the whole household.

September 21: Miss Prevost took us to call at Daviot; day rather cold and windy.

September 22: Wet, unpleasant day; called at Raigmore's to see Julia before her departure for London and the continent. Dined at Miss Jeannie's with Mr and Mrs Troughton, etc. Went to the steamer and saw Mr Troughton on board; saw Julia Mackintosh again and took leave.

September 23: Raining most of the day; thought of going to Polmaly, but gave it up.

September 24: Day wet and cold; nothing particular occurred.

September 25: A fine day; went to the Flower Show with Miss Prevost.

September 26: Very busy preparing sermon, etc., etc.

September 27 (Sunday, 15 Trinity): A miserable day with wind and rain. Chapel thinly attended; services good and music delightful. Went to the Fort in the evening and met D. Mackenzie junr. *[probably Duncan Mackenzie, incumbent at Arpafeelie]* who read prayers; returned to tea at Dr Munro's, where Mrs F. joined.

September 28: Wet day, went to the Infirmary with Miss Prevost.

September 29: Very wet and stormy; dined at Ness Cottage, and came to town in the carriage with Matilda and Aleck on their way to Balifeary.

September 30: Still wet (first day of the Northern Meeting).

October 1: Weather cleared up a little; walked to the Longman with Miss Prevost.; poured rain in the evening.

October 2: A fine day; walked to the race course *[at the Longman at that time – the races formed part of the Northern Meeting programme]* with the boys; Miss Prevost, Miss Shadwell and Matilda with us and Dr Munro.

October 3: Very busy all day in composing a sermon; dined with Miss Prevost and left at 7 o'clock.

October 4 (Sunday, 16 Trinity): Up at 6 in the morning, and went to Fort George; service there at half past 8 and returned for morning service here, was too late by nearly half an hour, the congregation being assembled. Chapel very full and, notwithstanding the excitement in the morning, everything was satisfactory. Mrs F. and I remained to dinner at Mr G. Anderson's and met General Mackenzie and his ladies.

October 5: Day a little showery; made several calls with Mrs F.

October 6: The same sort of weather, very unfavourable for the harvest. Miss Prevost and the Frasers and Miss Heliers went to the Fall of Foyers; called at Ness Cottage after tea.

October 7: Weather still wet; attended committee meeting at the Infirmary, etc., etc.

October 8: A dry day and much harvest work done.

October 9: A really beautiful day, and quite warm. Mr Murchison and Mr Macgillivray called in the forenoon, and Mrs F. and I dined with Miss Prevost, and walked home in lovely moonlight.

October 10: Very busy all day in writing a sermon; received an unexpected subscription for the Chapel from Mr Murchison. A beautiful day with some frost at night. Johnny went to Fort G. with Miss Prevost and Matilda Fraser.

October 11 (Sunday, 17 Trinity): A beautiful day with bright sunshine – a well-filled Church and music uncommonly good. Mr D. Mackenzie junr. officiated at Fort George.

October 12: A beautiful day; dined at Muirtown with a party to meet Miss Prevost.

October 13: Mrs [F.] and I went to Drumnadrochit with Miss Prevost and Matilda Fraser; we at Polmaly and they at the Inn, etc., etc.

October 14: Passed a delightful day in Glenurquhart and returned to Inverness in the afternoon and found all well.

October 15: Rained heavily all the forenoon; baptised Brodie of Brodie's son [father William, 1799–1873, Lord Lieut. of Nairnshire; son Hugh, 1840–1889, later Lord Lieut.] – large party in the Chapel on the occasion. Miss Prevost's last day with us, and had some friends to meet her – General Mackenzie, etc., etc.

October 16: Still rainy. Miss Prevost left for Aberdeen; Johnny accompanying her.

October 17: Day rather better; went to Nairn to read the burial office over the remains of Mr Clarke's third boy who died very suddenly. Reached home before six o'clock.

October 18 (Sunday, 18 Trinity): Went to Fort George at half past 6 in the morning; in time back for morning service at Inverness – a

79

very pleasing day. After evening service baptised a child of Mr Boulderson in Church. Mr H. Fraser, Struy, to dine with us.

October 19: Set off for Aberdeen per "Star" coach, Mrs F. going with me as far as Forres – slept at Elgin.

October 20: Proceeded to Aberdeen by the Mail; dined at Bishop Skinner's with Miss Prevost and Johnny, etc., etc. *[Bishop William Skinner (1778–1857), was the second son of Bishop John Skinner; William was elected Bishop of Aberdeen in 1816; he became Primus in 1841.]*

October 21: Settled about Johnny's lodgings in Old Aberdeen *[Johnny was then aged 16 and starting University]*, and went with Miss Prevost to Bridge of Don to the Old Cathedral College Chapel – dined with her and supped with Mr Frost.

October 22: Came as far as Huntly on my way home and spent a most pleasant evening at Mr Walker's.

October 23: Returned to Inverness per "Defiance".

October 24: Prayers in Chapel before Communion.

October 25 (Sunday, 19 Trinity): A fine day and a full Chapel – 61 communicants – a very satisfactory and I hope an edifying day.

October 25 *[an obvious error here, but no other day is omitted]*: Wet and cold; nothing particular happened.

October 26: Ditto, ditto; read the "British Critic" for October.

October 27: Hugh Fraser, Struy, breakfasted with us; a miserably cold and wet day. Snow for the first time on the Daviot hills.

October 28: Dined at Peter Anderson's to meet Hugh Fraser and the Ness-side family; a dry day for most part.

October 29: A beautiful day with bright sunshine.

October 30: Weather still fine; dined at Dr Munro's to meet General Mackenzie, Frasers, etc.

October 31: A beautiful day; nothing particular occurred.

November 1 (Sunday, 20 Trinity): A singularly interesting day altogether, the Chapel being crowded with Presbyterians both morning and evening; the effect of the Church services and sermons upon them seemed good. Day quite warm.

November 2: A lovely day; nothing occurred of much interest.

November 3: Day bright and warm; the municipal elections took place – declined to vote, against much solicitation *[Whigs became the majority in the Town Council, and were opposed to payment of the poor assessment, favoured by Fyvie]*.

November 4: Weather mild, but rained during the forenoon; attended meeting at the Infirmary, and afterwards Miss Macinnes's funeral. Read Knox and wrote letters in the evening.

November 5: Lady Mackenzie of Coul breakfasted with us; called on Miss Howard *[daughter of an English clergyman, probably Rev. J. Garton Howard, Vicar of St. Michael's, Derby, whose son became Secretary of the Clergy Friendly Society in 1882]* and took her to Mr Fraser's lodgings; day very beautiful and quite warm.

November 6: A beautiful day. Miss Howard dined with us; went to town with her in the evening and met her father.

November 7: Wrote a sermon for Sunday – very busy all day having various engagements – a lovely day.

November 8 (Sunday, 21 Trinity): Day very fine; Mr Howard read prayers in the morning; services well attended, singing a little ajar in the evening in consequence of xxxxx being absent on account of a sore throat.

November 9: Mr and Miss Howard dined with us, the weather clear and warm.

November 10: A most beautiful day. Matilda and John Fraser called after breakfast; walked into town with them and arranged about having their pew in Church covered.

November 11: Variously engaged in the forenoon, and Mrs *[F.]* and I dined in the evening at Dr Munro's to meet Mr and Miss Howard.

November 12: A very fine day, Matilda Fraser dined with *[?us]* quite alone; walked home with her part of the way under a beautiful sky and most brilliant moon.

November 13: Heavy gale from the north-east with rain. We were made uneasy from Mr and Mrs G. Anderson, etc., being on board the steamer on her passage to Leith *[a disastrous storm hit the Shetland Isles that day with great loss of life]*; in the evening dined at General Mackenzie with a party.

November 14: Busy with sermon, etc., as usual on Saturdays; day cold and wet.

November 15 (Sunday, 22 Trinity): Chapel very full; Mr Howard preached in the morning and went to Fort George to officiate in the afternoon. Read prayers and preached myself here to a large congregation. Took leave of Dr Munro who sets out for London in the morning of Monday – the steamer having put back, Mr and Mrs Anderson, Lady Mackinnon and the whole party were returned to Inverness; staid to dinner with them at Mr Anderson's and returned home early.

November 16: Dismal day of wind and rain without intermission. Mr Howard set out on his way to Derby.

November 17: Intensely cold, snow gradually getting nearer us, the hill of Dunain being well powdered while Wyvis is deeply inveloped [sic]; much occupied in writing letters, etc.

November 18: Very cold, but fair. Dined at Muirtown.

November 19: Day as to weather much as yesterday. Jamie [now aged 14] began to play the organ.

November 20: Fine November day; nothing particular occurred.

November 21: In the forenoon attended the funeral of Mr Phineas Mackintosh [of Ballifeary]. Rained most of the day; wrote a sermon for Sunday on the woman of Samaria [John iv.1-26].

November 22 (Sunday, last Trinity): A most pleasing and comfortable day, very full Chapel all day, and everything satisfactory; sermon much listened to; in the afternoon baptised Alexr. Macrae's child after the second lesson – the effect seemed impressive.

November 23: Weather continues beautiful. Mrs F. and I dined at Ness Cottage and walked home by the town at night.

November 24: The young party from Ness Cottage, Miss Howard and Miss Loader dined with us; day fresh and fair; in the forenoon had a meeting about settling Mr Smith's account for mason work of Chapel.

November 25: Nothing particular occurred; day beautiful.

November 26: Made satisfactory arrangements for settling Mr Smith's account; weather still beautiful.

November 27: Martinmas Market. A little frost in the morning, a bright sunshine all day, with frost at night.

November 28: A fine day, but cold and frosty towards night; occupied much as usual on Saturdays.

November 29 (Sunday, 1 Advent): A very <u>dark</u> day but soft and mild. Chapel remarkably full in the afternoon especially.

November 30: Nothing particular occurred. Met Mr Jones and Mr Hardie about Mr Smith's account for extra work in the mason work of the Chapel.

December 1: Weather cold and clear with frost at night.

December 2: Do., do., do. (nothing particular).

December 3: Thanksgiving for the Harvest; a dullish day, and Church not well attended which seems very surprising considering the great blessing of a good and plentiful harvest.

December 4: Fine open weather, with no frost. Called at Ness Cottage on my way from town.

December 5: Attended funeral of Mr Forbes of Culloden *[Duncan Forbes, 8th Laird of Culloden (1781–1840) – magistrate, deputy Lieutenant and a director of Inverness Royal Academy; died at Forres, aged 59, but was buried in the Chapel Yard, Inverness]* – an immense assemblage of people. Day mild and gloomy. Attended practising afterwards and returned home by 4 o'clock; had several interesting letters among which one from Mr Ramsay and one from Mr Hawthornthwaite.

December 6 (Sunday, 2 Advent): A mild, darkish day, a well-filled Church, and I trust an edified congregation; services remarkably well performed, without the slightest jar in the music and many thing beside (disagreeable circumstance about Mrs Campbell's pew).

December 7: Nothing particular occurred; wrote and received several letters.

December 8: Nothing happened deserving of notice.

December 9: A most beautiful day, bright sunshine and bracing air. Called at Leys Castle on the Whites. Mrs F. and I dined afterwards at Mr Pell's; came home rather under the most brilliant moonlight I ever saw; slight frost but not very cold.

December 10: Morning dark and rainy; called at Muirtown on Mrs Warrand; evening fine, and bright moonlight at night.

December 11: Dark December day and towards evening a dense

fog. Nothing particular occurred; called at Ness Cottage.

December 12: Engaged much as usual on Saturdays.

December 13 (Sunday, 3 Advent): A fair congregation forenoon and afternoon. Music very good and sermons very attentively listened to.

December 14: A very dismal, dark, rainy day; dined at Kingsmills.

December 15: Sudden change of weather, hard frost and clear atmosphere. Received a number of letters, one from Mr Copeland.

December 16: Wrote and forwarded a long letter to Bp. Low on the affairs of the Diocese; dined afterwards at Ness Cottage.

December 17: Weather changed to thaw; nothing particular occurred.

December 18: Soft day; busy all the forenoon in various ways. Went down to the ball given by the Academy boys *[an annual event]* for a little in the evening – pitch dark and some difficulty in keeping the road.

December 19: Employed much as usual on Saturdays.

December 20 (Sunday, 4 Advent): A very disagreeable day as to weather, raw, cold and dark. Chapel not very full. <u>My birth day</u> – Dr Munro returned from London, called for him on my way home from Church.

December 21: Nothing particular occurred; read Knox and made professional calls.

December 22: Clear with frost; engaged much as usual.

December 23: Beautiful winter weather, hard frost, made various calls. Mrs F. became unwell on coming home at 5 o'clock – very nervous and uncomfortable.

December 24: Mrs F. better, but not able to attend the service which was at 2 o'clock. Fine frosty day. Had a letter from Sir G. Prevost. Service very well attended; saw E. and M. Fraser afterwards in the vestry and had some conversation on religious subjects. Busy in the evening and Mrs F. I hope better.

December 25 (Christmas): Hard frost with fog and very cold. A very spirit-stirring day in a Christian sense. Church very well attended, and services quite delightful throughout – there were about 70 communicants. Mrs F. had a letter from Johnny. Dined at home quite alone. The chanting in the evening service most beautiful.

December 26: After morning prayers, administered the Sacrament to a sick person and made several professional calls in the evening, preparing as usual for Sunday (soft day).

December 27 (Sunday): A very cold disagreeable day, but tolerably well-filled Church; dined with Dr Munro.

December 28: Weather much the same, nothing particular.

December 29: Fine winter day; walked with Dr Munro to the ferry and back again, and talked a deal about our Church affairs.

December 30: Had a meeting of our Church building committee, and settled much important business with great and happy cordiality (surely God's blessing has been with us here). Cold disagreeable day, and not very well.

December 31: Miss Howard came to stay with us *[for]* a few days; nothing occurred worthy of notice. Heard from Margaret and Johnny and both well, and I trust doing well, <u>thank God</u>.

1841

January 1: Officiated at Fort George and administered the Holy Sacrament; returned in the evening and met Mrs Fyvie and Miss Howard at Raigmore's where we dined and spent the evening. Was much pleased to see a number of his small tenants and servants made happy at a New Year's Day dinner and little dance.

January 2: Busy as usual on Saturday; fine open day.

January 3 (Sunday): Heavy fall of snow during the night and snow fell most of the day. Chapel in consequence very thin. Collection for the Infirmary very good notwithstanding, amounting to £18.

January 4: Heavy snow almost the whole day; made calls; read Knox and wrote several letters.

January 5: Hard frost and much snow in the hills. Highland Mail upset at Dalmagarry on its way south, and no London mail arrived.

January 6: Frost and snow; nothing particular occurred. Reading Dr Pusey on Holy Baptism *[E. B. Pusey: "Scriptural Views of Holy Baptism", with the original edition in three parts published in 1834 – Pusey was a leader in the Oxford movement and writer of various tracts]*.

January 7: Thermometer at 18°*[F; –8°C]* in the morning; called at Ness Cottage on my way from town. We dined at Dr Munro's quite by ourselves.

January 8: Weather just the same; thermometer at 10°*[F; –12°C]*; during the night, but no more snow.

January 9: Frost continues; a mail still due; prepared for Sunday as usual.

January 10 (Sunday, 1 Epiphany): Dry, very cold, and Church rather thinly attended. Heard that Mackintosh had arrived in Morayshire. Services all satisfactory, but nothing particular occurred.

January 11: Snow storm still continues. Thermometer very low.

January 12: Snowing most of the day but a little softer. Reading the "British Critic" for January quarter.

January 13: Partly thaw, and very disagreeable walking.

January 14: Ditto,   ditto.

January 15: Freezing again, and very slippery. Dined at Ness

Cottage, where met Mr and Mrs Grant, Island Bank *[Inverness]*.

January 16: Dark softish day and about 9 at night began to rain torrents with high wind; occupied much as usual during the day. Letter from Johnny in Aberdeen. (Thermometer at 3° below 0°*[F; –19°C]*.)

January 17 (Sunday, 2 Epiphany): Very unpleasant day, rain <u>above</u> and ice <u>below</u> – no mail arrived from Edinburgh. Chapel very thinly attended, but services very good indeed.

January 18: Nothing particular occurred.

January 19: Do., do., weather still stormy and hard frost.

January 20: Clear frosty day; went in the afternoon to baptise Hon. Mr Fraser's infant daughter; dined there and returned in a post chaise at night.

January 21: A sudden thaw; pouring rain and roads all but impassable.

January 22: Ditto, ditto, with great departure of snow.

January 23: Sudden return to hard frost, with a heavy fall of snow during the night. Called for Mr Jones at Clachnaharry *[probably Thomas Jones, carpenter and lock-keeper on the Caledonian Canal]* who had been unwell; returned in time for practising in the Chapel. Sad account of Jackson's *[the organist]* journey to Tain – Sarah likely to be organist tomorrow.

January 24 (Sunday, Epiphany 3): A heavy fall of snow during the night and hard frost. Chapel rather thinly attended. Sarah played very well and music on the whole very satisfactorily good. Dr M. attended offertory for the first time.

January 25: Very cold during the day; at about 8 at night began to thaw, the air becoming perfectly mild, and snow disappeared very rapidly.

January 26: Snow nearly gone on the low grounds, and partially on the mountains; atmosphere uncommonly mild. Walked with Dr Munro to Clachnaharry to see Mr Jones whom we found getting better.

January 27: Occasional showers of rain with high winds. Had the bond signed for obtaining a loan on the Chapel. Dined at Ness Cottage and met Gen. Mackenzie, etc.; walked home by town and joined Mrs Fyvie at Dr Munro's.

January 28: Fine open weather, and snow off the low grounds; attended meeting in Gaelic Kirk about poor laws.

January 29: Mild weather; went with Miss Howard to look at Drakies House. Wrote to Mr Walker of Huntly about Mr Broderick's coming to Inverness as my Curate for a time. *[Wrote]* to Mr J. Skinner, W.S., inclosing a pound note and 3/6d stamp signed requesting to negotiate the bill on account of the organ; wrote several other letters.

January 30: Occupied much as usual on Saturdays. Had a letter from Mr Bowdler inclosing dividend of Lady Rosse's fund (note from Admiral Duff to Mrs F. very abominable). Discontinued Jackson's playing the organ.

January 31 (Sunday, 4 Epiphany): A fine day and a very good congregation both morning and evening. Sarah played very well, and the music very fairly good. Took leave of Mr Troughton who sets out tomorrow for England to see his son. Had a letter from Lord Saltoun intimating his wish to be a subscriber of £10 a year to the Scottish Episcopal Church Society.

February 1: Hard frost; walked to Stonyfield with Dr Munro and dined with him afterwards.

February 2: Attended meeting in the Gaelic Kirk about provision for the poor – voted for a legal assessment – a motion for a voluntary provision was carried, the subject being made one of party politics.

February 3: Frost, with easterly wind, intensely cold.

February 4: Nothing particular occurred. Miss Howard staying with us, prior to settling at Drakies *[where she set up a boarding school for upper-class girls, which soon failed due to the activities of the Italian lady whom she employed as an assistant]*.

February 5: Variously engaged; very cold with sharp easterly wind.

February 6: Occupied as usual on Saturdays. Miss Howard still with us; was amused with some of her anecdotes – the boy who on being asked 'who made him?' said 'I don't know, but I might rapp at *[= hazard]* a guess. I'm thinking it was Pontius Pilate.' Miss Howard's brother on going to a Curacy in a remote parish in Yorkshire where dissenters were very numerous was much shocked with the opinions and habits prevalent among the parishioners – on the first Sunday he officiated, just after the blessing, and while he was at his private devotions, a man got up and said 'Samy Hardacre is to preach at 2 o'clock in such and such a place.'

February 7 (Sunday, Septuagesima): Frost and very cold – Chapel pretty full notwithstanding and services satisfactory; after service went to see Miss Ogilvie at Mr Scott's; had several interesting letters.

February 8: Nothing particular – hard frost.

February 9: Do., do., do. Poor Miss Ogilvie becoming quite insane.

February 10: Princess Royal baptised *[Princess Victoria, born 21st November 1840; later married Prince Frederick of Prussia and in 1861 became Crown Princess of Prussia]*; hard frost and very cold.

February 11: Dined at Dr Munro's; reading "Life of *[Mr Henry]* Dodwell" *[Francis Brokesby, 1715 and later editions]*.

February 12: Wrote and received several letters; fine thaw.

February 13: As usual on Saturdays.

February 14 (Sunday, Sexagesima): Church rather full and services very satisfactory. Sarah greatly improving in playing. Had afternoon prayers at quarter before 2 o'clock, and went to Fort George afterwards; officiated there at half past three, and baptised Capt. Sampson's child and read two churching services *[a service where a blessing is given to a woman following childbirth]*. Returned home a little past 8; night dark and pouring rain and the roads nave deep *[= up to the hub of a wheel]*. Miss Howard and G. Anderson dined with Mrs Fyvie at Roseheath.

February 15: Bright sunshine, soft and spring-like; walked to Ness Cottage on my way to town.

February 16: A beautiful day; dined at Mr G. Anderson's and met Dr Munro; walked home by Kingsmills for Mrs F. who dined there.

February 17: Weather continued fine and we dined at Muirtown, Jamie and Charlie coming to tea; walked home pretty early.

February 18: Nothing particular occurred.

February 19: A very fine day, fresh and blowing from the south. I dined at Ness Cottage, and Mrs F. and the boys at Muirtown. Mrs Warrand not very well from sore throat.

February 20: As usual on Saturdays; practising, etc., etc.

February 21 (Sunday, Quinquagesima): A very good congregation and a fine day. Music particularly good and Sarah improving vastly in playing the organ. Mrs F. confined from rheumatism; Miss Howard dined at Roseheath.

February 22: A beautiful day and nothing particular occurred; heard that Mrs R. Macfarlane was dangerously ill.

February 23: Went to Earlsmills in Morayshire to see Mackintosh of Mackintosh; weather quite like summer.

February 24 (Ash Wednesday): Prayers much better attended than usual, the day being very fine.

February 25: Called at Muirtown; day something cold; Mrs F. confined chiefly to her room.

February 26: Very cold day, but fair; dined at Mrs Macgillivray's, Dunmaglass, with En*[eas]* Mackintosh, John Fraser, Matilda and Alexr.

February 27: Had a letter from Rev. C. Birch intimating the death of Mrs R. Macfarlane. Quiescat in Pace *[= May he/she rest in peace]*, Amen.

February 28 (Sunday, 1 Lent): Fine day and very good congregation both services; went to Fort George at 3 after two services here; officiated there and returned at 9 dreadfully knocked up.

March 1: Nothing particular; cold easterly wind.

March 2: Do.,   do.

March 3: Heard of the death of Madame Roy *[identity not known]* at Paris.

March 4: Nothing particular occurred.

March 5: An uncomfortable day in many respects.

March 6: Occupied as usual on Saturdays. The screen in front of the organ nearly finished.

March 7 (Sunday, 2 Lent): A fine day, and Chapel pretty well filled. Heard of the death of Bishop *[James]* Walker *[Bishop of Edinburgh 1830–1841 and Primus 1837–1841]* who expired at 8 o'clock on Friday the 5th. Dined with Mr G. Anderson; nothing particular in the services.

March 8: A fine day – walked to Muirtown with Dr Munro to call for Mrs Warrand. Mrs W. walked with us about the garden; went to Inverness in the evening to attend a concert.

March 9: Weather very fine; nothing particular occurred.

March 10: Prayers in Chapel at half past eleven; took a drive afterwards with Mrs F. as far as Dochfour; quite like summer weather. New house at Dochfour on a great scale *[home of the Baillies of Dochfour, greatly extended in 1839 and modified into an Italianate mansion by William Robertson of Elgin, who also designed St. John's Church in the same year]*.

March 11: Warm and full of sunshine as to the world without, but otherwise I am under a course of worry in various respects, yet, D.G., not without hope.

March 12: With the heat and brightness of June, went to town early – received notification of the death of Henry Stuart of Ballachulish (on the 8th inst.). Called at Ness Cottage, and walked about the grounds and on the Drummond Hill with Eliza*[?]*, Matilda, etc.

March 13: Occupied as usual on Saturdays.

March 14 (Sunday, 3 Lent): A beautiful day, and Church rather full; went to Fort George to officiate after both services at Inverness; came home about 8 o'clock, and to return to the Fort tomorrow to bury a soldier of the Royals.

March 15: Went to Fort George to bury the soldier; remained to dinner and returned in the evening. A most lovely day, bright sun and warm south wind.

March 16: Weather equally beautiful; dined at Raigmore's and met Lady Anne and Mr James Mackenzie of Scatwell.

March 17: Dined again at Raigmore's; made several calls in the forenoon after morning prayers; weather like June.

March 18: Nothing particular occurred.

March 19: Sale of United Charities Buildings, which have occasioned me so much trouble and expense. Weather beautiful, with rather high wind. Mr G. Anderson walked up with me and dined with us.

March 20: As usual on Saturdays; wind rather boisterous, with slight showers occasionally, but not cold. Wrote to Johnnie and sent him a Post Office order for £5 to pay the balance of his expenses at College.

March 21 (Sunday, 4 Lent): Very high wind during the night; morning bright and fine. Church very well attended, and services quite satisfactory – music very good. Letter from Maggie, who is with Miss Prevost at Leamington.

March 22: Nothing particular. Daffodils full blown under the hedge; a good deal employed in the garden.

March 23: All forenoon in the garden; went to the Chapel at 4 to baptise a child; at 6 dined at Dr Munro's to meet General Mackenzie. Fine March weather.

March 24: After morning prayers, attended meeting of Infirmary Directors, and during the remainder of the day variously occupied. Day bright and fine. Reading Mr Newman's Tract No. 90 Oxford Tracts. *["Remarks on Certain Passages in the Thirty-Nine Articles" by John Henry Newman, published in 1841, is the most famous and the most controversial of the "Tracts for the Times" produced by the first generation of the Anglo-Catholic Oxford Movement.]*

March 25: Engaged about sale of ground behind the Chapel.

March 26: Concluded a sale of the ground with Mr Thomson, Banker, for £300.

March 27: Attended meeting about proposed Market on the ground behind the Chapel; practising, etc.; a beautiful day with fine showers in the morning.

March 28 (Sunday, 5 Lent): A comfortable day and services satisfactory; went to the Fort in the evening as usual; weather continues beautiful.

March 29: Johnny returned from College; much improved apparently.

March 30: Nothing particular occurred.

March 31: D. Mackenzie junr. read prayers. Attended a meeting at Infirmary afterwards; easterly wind and rather cold (dined at the Dunmaglass's).

April 1: Heavy rain most of the forenoon; very beneficial to vegetation, tho' rather cold (thermometer 41°*[F; 5°C]*).

April 2: Nothing particular occurred; most of the forenoon employed in the garden.

April 3: Employed as usual on Saturdays; day rather cold with occasional showers; fresh snow on Wyvis. Alex and *[sentence finishes here and duplicates start of next entry]*

April 4 (Sunday before Easter): Nothing particular in the services but all right and Chapel pretty full. Received a letter from Mr Ferguson of St. Peter's, Edinburgh, announcing that Mr [Charles] Terrot had been elected as the new Bishop of Edinburgh in room [= place] of Bp. Walker, and that it is understood Bp. Skinner would be Primus.

April 5: Prayers in Chapel at eleven; much occupied the rest of the forenoon in professional calls, etc.; after dinner worked in the planting, and by moonlight in the garden with Jamie until quarter past nine – a more lovely night I never beheld. Johnny dined at Kingsmills. Wrote to Mr Murdoch with a [bank] draft for £6 from Lady Rosse's fund; also to Mr Ferguson.

April 6: Prayers in Chapel; rest of the day employed much as yesterday.

April 7: After Morning Prayers delivered a lecture from the reading desk; professional calls afterwards. Weather showery but not cold.

April 8: Delivered a lecture again after Morning Prayers as yesterday – a considerable number attended Church; in the evening finished my sermon for Good Friday. Latter part of the day rather cold, with occasional showers. Called at Gen. Mackenzie's for Mrs Robertson, Kindeace [near Invergordon]; heard of Margaret from Miss Prevost at Leamington.

April 9 (Good Friday): A fine day. Preached in the forenoon from "As Moses lifted up the serpent in the wilderness, etc." [John iii.4]. Baptised a child between services. Prayers at 2 o'clock very well attended. Made several professional calls afterwards. In the evening began sermon for Easter Day.

April 10: Very much occupied all the day; wrote a sermon for Easter Day. Afternoon service at 3 p.m. very well attended; practising at 2.

April 11 (Easter): A very comfortable and cheering day. Services beautiful and music uncommonly good and steady. (Sarah as firm as a rock, and so exceedingly correct.) Sermon very attentively listened to. Chapel very well filled and 81 communicants. Had unlooked-for assistance from Mr Melville, Lord Ward's Chaplain, who assisted at the altar and read prayers in the afternoon. Lord Ward and the Marquess of Blandford [John Spencer-Churchill, later 7th Duke of Marlborough, and paternal grandfather of Sir Winston Churchill] were in Church.

April 12: After Morning Prayers and a sermon in Church, made various professional calls, and returned home via Ness Cottage to enquire for Matilda who has been prevented from being in Church by an attack of influenza; weather bright and fine.

April 13: Day rather cold. We dined at Gen. Mackenzie's to meet Mrs Robertson of Kindeace.

April 14: Nothing particular occurred.

April 15: Ditto.   Fine weather.

April 16: Circuit Court sitting; received a letter from Mr Tyrwhitt about his coming to assist me and to be tutor in Hon. Mr Fraser's family.

April 17: Occupied as usual on Saturdays; towards evening it became very cold.

April 18 (Sunday, 1 Easter): Violent wind and rain throughout the whole day with only occasional blinks of sunshine. Chapel rather thinly attended in consequence; baptised two children between services.

April 19: Administered the communion to some sick people and visited others.

April 20: Weather rather cold, with snow on the mountains.

April 21: Weather continues rather cold; nothing particular.

April 22: Do.,   do.

April 23: Sowed annuals and did other work in the garden.

April 24: Occupied as usual on Saturdays; weather becoming milder.

April 25 (Sunday, 2 Easter): A fine day but with high wind. Church fairly attended, but nothing particular.

April 26: Nothing particular occurred.

April 27: Ditto,   ditto.

April 28: Weather suddenly become very warm; letter from A. Duff to Mrs [F.] and myself, to which replied by evening post. Finished sewing annuals in the garden. Matilda came to us to stay a few days.

April 29: Weather fine, but wind easterly.

April 30: Some fine rain towards the afternoon. Æneas Macintosh, David and Miss Jeannie dined with us.

May 1: Rained heavily most of the day. Matilda returned home before tea; occupied as usual Saturdays.

May 2 (Sunday, 3 Easter): A very cold day with occasional showers of snow, and high wind from the north-east. Chapel rather thinner than usual in consequence; the music very good indeed.

May 3: Cold, with torrents of rain from morning till night, with but few intermissions. A good deal of vexatious kind of business to struggle with.

May 4: Still cold and rainy. Wrote to Mr Dalton of Wolverhampton.

May 5: Temperature suddenly changed, southerly wind and quite warm without bright sunshine. Did a good deal of work in the garden with the boys. Despatched a Memorial to the Treasury praying for the drawback on the wood and glass employed in the Chapel *[this was later refused as it was not the policy of the Church Commissioners to grant certificates for allowances of drawback on materials used in building and enlarging Episcopal churches in Scotland – the reply survives in the Church records]*. Wrote also to the Chaplain General about New Year's Day service at Fort-George.

May 6: Very fine day. Mrs Minty and Barbara Paterson dined with us. Peter Anderson, Mrs P. Anderson, Mrs J. Anderson and Mary to tea.

May 7: Nothing particular occurred.

May 8: A perfectly summer day; went early into town to church Mrs Enderby; practising afterwards, and other duties, much as usual on Saturdays; at night occupied in completing preparations for Sunday.

May 9 (Sunday, 4 Easter): Upon the whole a satisfactory day. Beautiful weather but the prevailing influenza and illness among children affecting Church attendance. Marianne Watson prayed for as in a dying state.

May 10: Nothing particular occurred.

May 11: Ditto,   ditto.

May 12: Negotiating about sale of old Chapel. Reading Robertson's "History of Charles XII" *[an error – should be "History of Charles V" by William Robertson (1721–1793) – see August 18 below]* and part of Bp. Horsley's works *[Samuel Horsley, successively Bishop of St. David's, Rochester and St. Asaph's]*.

May 13: Most beautiful weather; employed much the same as yesterday; went down to Ness Cottage in the evening.

May 14: Much the same sort of day, and employed much in the same way.

May 15: Much as usual on Saturdays; dry and windy in point of weather, and without any incidents of the slightest interest. It is thought [that] the Whigs are at last to walk out of office, a thing hard to be believed. The Corn Law interposed by them I supposed is meant to create commiseration as corns are known to be very much against locomotion of any kind.

May 16 (Sunday, 5 Easter): An agreeable day upon the whole, and services quite satisfactory; preached twice on spiritual influences, sermons suitable for the season which were very attentively listened to; walked with the boys in the evening in the direction of Leys.

May 17: Nothing particular occurred; weather fine.

May 18: Ditto,   ditto.

May 19: A little showery; walked to the Ferry and back with Dr Munro, and afterwards dined with him at Viewmount.

May 20 (Ascension Day): Very few attended prayers. Pease in blossom.

May 21: Nothing particular occurred; very beautiful weather.

May 22: Very hot day; occupied much as usual on Saturdays; a capital practising.

May 23 (Sunday after Ascension): An exceedingly hot day. Chapel very well filled and services satisfactory. Mrs Troughton returned from England. Walked with the boys to the heights above Parks in the evening.

May 24: Warm and dry; walked with the boys to the top of the hill of Dunain.

May 25: Very warm and very dry; transacted a good deal of important business.

May 26: Extremely hot day; occupied with giving and receiving money more than I like to be.

May 27: Extremely hot day.

May 28: Intense heat; made some pastoral calls, etc.

May 29: Very hot. Prayers at 3 in the afternoon, followed by a lecture on "The Feeding in the Desert". Chants sung by the choir with good effect. At night very annoying adventure with tinkers and blackguards about the place, and kept up till 2 in the morning.

May 30 (Whitsunday): A beautiful day, and Chapel cheeringly full (60 communicants) – the impression on the whole very pleasing, and the result I hope profitable to us all. Mrs F. and I intend setting out for Aberdeen at 2 tomorrow morning.

May 31: Mrs F. and I started by by the mail at 2 in the morning and arrived at Peterhead at 8 p.m., all safe, D.G. Saw the new Chapel at Portsoy, etc.; passed through Banff and the district of Buchan.

June 1: Walked around Peterhead all the forenoon and saw several very old acquaintances; at quarter past 6 in the afternoon left Mrs F. at a lodging for bathing and proceeded to Aberdeen where I arrived at 11.

June 2: Was present at the consecration of Bishop Terrot *[new Bishop of Edinburgh]*. All the Bishops assisted in the service which was very impressive. Honble. Mr York *[Grantham Munton Yorke, who became Dean of Worcester in 1874]* preached from Hebrews xiii.17 *[Obey your leaders and submit to them, for they are keeping watch over your souls, as men who will have to give account]*. Dined at Bp. Skinner's afterwards with them; wrote to Mrs F. at Peterhead.

June 3: In the morning went to see St. Paul's Chapel and organ *[on the west side of the Gallowgate, and built around 1721 – it had a magnificent organ, of which a photograph exists; chapel demolished about 1865 and replaced by a Gothic structure]*. At 12 started for Huntly and arrived there at 5, thus overtaking Bishop Low who had gone on at 6 in the morning; slept at Mr Walker's.

June 4: Proceeded per mail to Inverness, leaving Bp. Low at Keith; found all well; wrote to Mrs F. on my arrival.

June 5: Married Dr Cruickshank and Miss Marlow in Church at quarter before 10 o'clock – this was the first time the marriage ceremony was performed in the new Church. Dined at Ness Cottage; wrote to Mrs F.

June 6 (Trinity Sunday): A rather cold day. Mr D. Mackenzie junr. preached in the forenoon, a very good sermon and not ill delivered. Read the "Si Quis" *[= if any one – a notification by a candidate for ordination asking if any impediment may be alleged against him]* for the deacons about to be ordained at Highfield Chapel *[Muir of Ord]*, and announced the confirmation on the 20th; preached in the afternoon a sermon appropriate for the day. Dined at Dr Munro's and returned home early. Wrote to Mrs F.

June 7: Went to Elgin by the "Star" coach and joined Bp. Low.

June 8: Passed the early part of the day in Elgin and went to visit the Cathedral with Mr Douglas; came on to Forres with the Bp. and Mr D. in the afternoon and slept there.

June 9: Returned to Inverness in the forenoon; dined at Dr Munro's. Mrs F. returned by the mail in the evening.

June 10: Passed a quiet day at home with a friend or two to dine with the Bishop. A very hot day.

June 11: Went with the Bp. to Highfield and preached at the ordination of the 3 Mackenzies – Duncan of Fortrose being ordained Priest, and his brother Kenneth and cousin Duncan, deacons – a very satisfactory day altogether. Returned with Johnny at night in the carriage that took us over in the morning, and joined Mrs F. at Dunmaglass.

June 12: Passed a very unpleasant day. + +

June 13 (Sunday 1 Trinity): A fine day and pretty full Church, but nothing particular occurred.

June 14: Passed a most particularly unhappy day.

June 15: Crossed the Kessock Ferry and met the Bishop at Allan Bank *[Black Isle]*; took Jamie along with me to take a drawing of the Chapel at Arpafeelie; returned a little after six, very tired.

June 16: Rain beautifully warm and fine, and towards evening quite fair. Occupied in examining candidates for confirmation, etc., etc. Expect to see the Bp. tomorrow and have asked some friends to meet him.

June 17: Bishop and Mr Douglas arrived in the forenoon; occupied in examining candidates for confirmation. Had a pretty large party at dinner and had new potatoes from our own garden for the first time.

June 18: Dined at Dr Munro's with the Bishop.

June 19: Very warm day, dined at Dunmaglass's with the Bishop and a pretty large party. Mr Douglas, having gone to Urquhart on Friday, did not arrive till the evening.

June 20 (Sunday, 2 Trinity): The Bishop preached in the forenoon and confirmed 13 young persons. I preached in the afternoon, and read prayers forenoon and afternoon. On the whole this has been a satisfactory day. Jamie played the organ in the afternoon, Sarah having been taken ill.

June 21: Went to Strathnairn with the Bishop, Mrs F. and all the boys also. Dined at Farr and returned in the evening.

June 22: Very warm day; walked to Clava with Mr Douglas and returned to Daviot to dinner and joined the Bp., Mrs. F., etc., etc. and returned in the evening.

June 23: Held a meeting of our Diocesan committee in the forenoon. Went to see the exhibition of flowers in Bell's Institution *[in Farraline Park, now used as Inverness Library]*. The Bp., Mr Maclauren, Mr Douphrate and others dined with us; day warm and showery.

June 24: The Bishop and Mr Douglas took their departure for Fort William; showery with a good deal of thunder.

June 25: Nothing particular occurred; <u>we all</u> dined at Dunmaglass's.

June 26: Occupied as usual on Saturdays. Nothing particular occurred.

June 27 (Sunday, 3 Trinity): Sacrament in the Kirk. A very warm day, and Church pretty full in the forenoon, and sermons greatly listened to and I hope profitably by many. Music exceedingly good. Intend to set out for Ballachulish tomorrow to attend the Bishop's visitation.

June 28: Mrs F. and I slept at Mrs Strachan's and at 5 in the morning set off by steam boat for Fort William. Day wet and company various (Lord and Lady Lovat and family, etc., etc.); slept at Mr Macgregor's and spent —

June 29: — the following day at Fort William very agreeably.

June 30: Mr Macgregor drove me in his gig to Ballachulish. Joined the Bishop and clergy at the Chapel at 11 o'clock. Rev. Mr Pritchard *[later spelling is Prichard – not identified]* read prayers and Mr Douphrate preached the visitation sermon ("We preach Christ crucified" *[1Cor. i.23]*); the Bishop's charge afterwards. The Bishop as usual had all the clergy and a few lay gentlemen to dine with him at the inn. Returned to Fort William in the evening.

July 1: A fine day which we spent quietly at Fort William.

July 2: Set out for Inverness at 8 o'clock in a carr *[a two-wheeled carriage drawn by a horse]*, and with a most lovely day. Took up Mr Greig *[incumbent at Caroy in Skye, 1838–1846]* at Fort Augustus; left the carr at Drumnadrochit and took another conveyance and reached Inverness a little after midnight (slept at Mrs Strachan's).

July 3: Very busy the whole day in various ways.

July 4 (Sunday, 4 Trinity): Heavy rain all the morning and forenoon, and thin Church in consequence; nothing particular occurred, but the day has left an unpleasing impression.

July 5: Rainy and cold.

July 6: Do., do.

July 7: Deluges of rain all day; went to Muirtown Locks to meet the Bp. and Mr Prichard and Mr Woolcombe [not identified].

July 8: Cold and rainy; went to see the Panorama of Jerusalem with Dr Munro [probably a touring version of Robert Burford's "Description of a View of the City of Jerusalem" (1841)].

July 9: Do., do. (Wool market).

July 10: Still rainy and cold; snow on Wyvis.

July 11 (Sunday, 5 Trinity): Mr Woolcombe read prayers in the morning and Mr Prichard preached, the Bp. and I taking the altar service. In the afternoon, I read prayers, and Mr Prichard preached again; the Bp. and the clergy and a very few friends besides dined with us. A very pleasing and I hope a profitable day.

July 12: A very wet day; dined with the Bishop, Mr Prichard, etc., at Dunmaglass's.

July 13: Very rainy all day. Baptised an adult in the Chapel, the Bp. confirmed immediately after; dined and slept at Dr. M's.

July 14: Set out at 6 in the morning with the Bp., etc., etc. to Forres to assist at the consecration of the Chapel there; after the consecration was over we proceeded to Elgin where we slept at the inn; continued rain all day.

July 15: Our party visited the ruins of the Cathedral in the early part of the day; lunched afterwards at Mrs Foljambe's; and in the afternoon Mr Prichard and I returned by the "Defiance" coach to Roseheath. Heavy rain most of the way.

July 16: Weather cleared up; Mr Prichard and Johnny went to Daviot for the day – I in town variously occupied.

July 17: Read funeral service at interment of Miss [Hannah] Dealtry [aged 72], and employed afterwards as usual on Saturdays.

July 18 (Sunday, 6 Trinity): A fine day and Chapel well attended; Mr Prichard preached in the morning and I in the afternoon. A very pleasing and I hope profitable day.

July 19: Wet, wet, wet. Mr Prichard left us and Johnny went to Polmaly for a week.

July 20: Still raining.

July 21: Attended examination of *[Inverness Royal]* Academy, etc., etc.

July 22: Heavy rain, still nothing particular.

July 23: Weather partially cleared up; had a letter from Mr Drummond announcing that the Bishop of Virginia was to be in Inverness on Saturday and Sunday *[probably Rt. Rev. Richard Channing Moore]*.

July 24: In the forenoon much as usual on Saturdays; waited the Bp. of Virginia's arrival and arranged that he was to preach on Sunday in the forenoon.

July 25 (Sunday 7 Trinity): This has been a remarkable spirit-stirring day. I read in the morning and the Bishop preached a capital sermon. Mr Stowell of Manchester was in Church both morning and evening, but declined preaching in consequence of a complaint in the throat. In the afternoon Mr Hopper from Worcester read prayers and Mr Ewing preached. The services were all good and after the evening service a young lady from Surrey introduced herself and requested to be allowed a copy of our "Te Deum" as she said she had never heard anything so beautiful. She was a Miss Russel. I gave her the music and had a nice note from her in the evening. The Bp. and Mr Hooper dined with us, and in the evening we all joined Mr Stowell's party at the Union Hotel, where there was an evening service and a lecture by Mr Stowell; remarkably good.

July 26: Showery day. Mr Stowell and his party went to Kilmorack in the forenoon, and returned to us, to tea.

July 27: Continued rain; made several calls and wrote to Bp. Low.

July 28: Weather just the same; sent £5 to old Mr Paterson by his daughter.

July 29: Day very rainy. Miss J. Mackintosh taken very ill; wrote to Mrs Troughton about her state; heard of J. Troughton's arrival.

July 30: A cold, unpleasant day; past *[sic]* most of it *[in]* town, having remained to dine with Mrs Troughton, Mr Troughton, etc. at Miss Mackintosh's, she being much better.

July 31: Still wet and disagreeable; Mrs Warrand and her children dined with us, also Mr Gordon from Fraserburgh.

August 1 (Sunday, 8 Trinity): A fair day but rather chilly. Mr Troughton read prayers forenoon and afternoon; Mr Ewing read the epistle and I preached twice.

August 2: Day nearly fair, but everything looking drenched.

August 3: A few hours of sunshine; wrote a great many letters. Paid the half-yearly interest on the bond over the Chapel – £15.6.6.

August 4: Was introduced to Rev. T. Alves, and drove with Mrs Fyvie and him first to Muirtown and then to Seabank to see Mrs xxxxx.

August 5: Heavy rain again; called at Ness Cottage on way to town, where I met the sad tidings of poor Jane Duff's death at Madras on the 8th June. Mrs F. went to Mrs Warrand in the afternoon, and I afterwards; we walked home late, under heavy rain.

August 6: Rain still continues. Mr Alves breakfasted with us, and I went to town and made several calls and afterwards to Muirtown to see Mrs Warrand.

August 7: Arrival of Rev. Mr Dodds, who took tea with us. Prayers in Chapel at 2 p.m.; day fair for most part, but heavy rain in the evening.

August 8 (Sunday, 9 Trinity): A very delightful day in every respect, Mr Alves read morning prayers and Mr Dodds and I took the Altar service, and Mr Troughton preached. In the afternoon Mr Dodds read prayers and I preached. There were 70 communicants. Mr Dodds, Mr Troughton, etc., dined with us.

August 9: A tremendous storm of thunder; was at Muirtown at the time with Mrs Warrand – large hailstones fell there and the lightning was most vivid. The storm continued more than an hour. There was neither rain nor hail at Roseheath.

August 10: Cold, showery day; nothing particular occurred.

August 11: Still rains; went in the evening to Muirtown with Mrs F. to see Mrs Warrand.

August 12: Weather considerably cleared. Johnny returned from Duffus, and Mrs Maclachlan from Elgin by the "Defiance"; called on Mrs Bushe (Miss Noel) [professional singer] with Sarah and Lydia.

August 13: Still wet occasionally through the day.

August 14: Very rainy; Mrs Bushe attended practising and sung most beautifully; wrote a sermon for Sunday.

August 15 (Sunday 10 Trinity): Did the whole duty forenoon and afternoon – a good congregation, and a very interesting day altogether. Music capital notwithstanding Donald's absence. Mrs F. confined all day with a bad cold.

August 16: A dry day; dined at Ness Cottage; occupied most of the forenoon in making professional calls and writing letters. Heavy rain in the evening.

August 17: Rainy; nothing particular occurred.

August 18: Shocking account of Sp___ Res___ *[meaning not identified]*; wrote several letters and finished reading "Charles V"; all dined at Dunmaglass's. Mrs Maclachlan still with us.

August 19: Day particularly dry; "North Star" steamer stranded at Fort George (telescope at the Castle).

August 20: Fair with high wind during the forenoon and heavy rain about 6 in the evening. Reading xxxx xxxx.

August 21: Very rainy day; extremely busy all day and dined at Mrs Strachan's to save time; went in the evening to the steam boat to meet Mr Bridges.

August 22 (Sunday, 11 Trinity): Mr Bridges preached twice. In the afternoon Mr Bethune read prayers. The Chapel was very full, and the services quite beautiful; Mrs Bushe sang.

August 23: Uncommonly heavy rain during the night; in the forenoon rather fair. Dined at Raigmore's with Mr Bridges, etc. Exposition, prayers, etc. there at night; took Mr Drummond in our carriage.

August 24: Meeting in the Chapel for Church Missionary Society – delivered a short address. Mr Drummond, Mr *[E.]* Walford of Dallingho *[Suffolk]* and Mr Bridges spoke at great length; audience rather small and collection only £14 . 2/-.

August 25: A fine day. Harriet Mackintosh of Farr called and took an early dinner. Mr Maclachlan afterwards went with her to Flichity *[Strathnairn]* to spend a few days.

August 26: A beautiful day; bright and cheering. Unexpected arrival of Mr Trevellyan about 12 o'clock; went to town with him and visited the Chapel, along with Mr More, etc., etc. Dined at Mrs Strachan's; all of us went to Muirtown to tea. This has been a very singularly interesting day of varied incident.

August 27: A painful kind of day. + Dined at Raigmore's, and first heard of Sophia's marriage to Mr Freeman.

August 28: Most of the forenoon in Chapel; beautiful practising. Mrs Bushe sung "Ye lympid springs, etc." *[an aria from act 3 of George Frideric Handel's oratorio "Jephtha"]*, Julia Mackenzie, Eneas, etc., sitting on the floor of the Chancel. Mr Trevellyan dined with us.

August 29 (Sunday 12 Trinity): A glorious day, Mr Trevellyan said prayers and preached in the morning, Mr Troughton and I at the altar. In the evening Mr Troughton preached and Mr *[J.]* Wilson of Corpus Christi College, Oxford, said prayers; the music most admirable. Mr Trevellyan and Mr Wilson dined with us, Mrs Maclachlan, do.

August 30: A very fine day; nothing particular occurred.

August 31: Went to Kilmuir for a few day's bathing, i.e. Mrs F. and I, Johnny and Jamie.

September 1: Walked about Kilmuir, Ord of Kessock, Munlochy Bay, etc. Surprised at the beauty of the scenery.

September 2: Crossed over to Inverness in a boat under very heavy rain; found a card from Rev. G. R. Gleig *[son of Bishop of Brechin; at that time Chaplain to Chelsea Hospital, later Chaplain-General of the Forces]*; walked over to Raigmore's to tea.

September 3: Mrs Fyvie, Jamie and Charlie went *[to]* Kilmuir in a boat.

September 4: Mrs F. and the two boys returned from Kilmuir; occupied as usual on a Saturday; some very heavy showers.

September 5 (Sunday, 13 Trinity): Mr Troughton said prayers morning and evening, and I preached twice. Expected Mr Gleig up from Fort George before Church time, but he did not arrive. Mr Gleig arrived to dinner – Raigmore, G. Anderson, Rev. Mr Southouse, Dr Munro, etc., to tea.

September 6: Dined at Miss Howard's to meet Mr and Mrs Southouse, Mr and Mrs Thomson, etc.; nothing particular occurred during the day.

September 7: Went all to Kilmuir; heard that Dr *[Basil]* Tytler *[aged about 26, nephew of Sheriff Fraser-Tytler]* had been drowned when fishing in the river.

September 8: Crossed from Kilmuir to Inverness and returned in the evening.

September 9: Crossed from Kilmuir to do some business; met Mr Thos. Gipps *[Church of England clergyman]* at the ferry; dined with Mr G. Anderson and returned to Kilmuir under a very dark sky.

September 10: Crossed to Inverness with Charlie, and made several calls in town before going to Roseheath; dined at Lady Saltoun's with the intention of sleeping at Ness Cottage, but Mrs F. and the other boys having come over also in the evening, I returned to Roseheath and found Mrs. F. very ill of rheumatism.

September 11: A beautiful day, and very busy during the whole of it; had a long interview with Mr W. Forbes, Lord Medwyn's son *[Lord Medwyn was a Scottish judge; two of his sons became Episcopalian clergymen]*; practising as usual, etc., etc.

September 12 (Sunday, 14 Trinity): A total change of weather – excessively hot and bright. A full church and all I trust to edification; had no assistance.

September 13: Extremely hot day, went to Aldourie to consecrate a burying ground. Mr and Mrs Southouse returned from Forres to dinner. Aleck and John Fraser to tea.

September 14: Excessive heat – thermometer 80°*[F; 27°C]* in the shade; called at Raigmore's to make arrangements about Sophia's marriage.

September 15: Went to Aldourie to read burial office over the remains of Dr Tytler whose body was found in the river. Stopped to dine at Ness Cottage. Continued heat.

September 16: Married Mr Freeman and Sophia Mackintosh in the Chapel, when there was a very numerous attendance. In the evening went to Mrs Bushe's concert.

September 17: Nothing particular occurred; crossed the ferry and called at Redcastle, and on the way home dined at Craigton Cottage, having gone so far to meet Johnny on his way from Kilmuir; returned in the evening.

September 18: As usual on Saturdays; a fine day.

September 19 (Sunday 15 Trinity): A beautiful day and a good congregation; had the duty myself. Dr Munro dined with us.

September 20: Fine harvest weather; called at Muirtown, etc., etc.

September 21: Fine weather. Mrs F. confined with rheumatism.

September 22: Mrs F. still confined to bed with rheumatism; did not go to town till after 8 at night.

September 23: Mrs F. still confined with rheumatism.

September 24: Fine weather and much harvest work done.

September 25: Completed a sermon for Sunday from "What do ye more than others" *[Matt. v.47]*. Mrs F. much better.

September 26 (Sunday 16 Trinity): A full congregation and services all quite smooth and beautiful. Mr and Mrs Macgillivray were in Church in the evening, this being likely to be their last Sunday in the country. Sermon listened to with great attention.

September 27: An uncomfortable day in many respects.

September 28: Mr Fraser of Struy breakfasted with us; I walked to Daviot to dinner, Mrs F. being unable to go. Met a party there and returned at night with Miss Mackintosh, Holm.

September 29: A fine day with no particular incident; made various calls, etc., etc.

September 30: Northern Meeting proceedings going forward and passed considerable part of the day in making arrangements for horticultural show in the *[Royal]* Academy hall *[in Academy Street]*, and dined at Mr G. Anderson's.

October 1: Horticultural show, with a rather favourable day.

October 2: Pouring rain; attended Mrs Bushe's concert and finished a sermon for Sunday.

October 3 (Sunday, 17 Trinity): A full Chapel and all satisfactory; baptised a child during the evening service; rather cold.

October 4: A fine harvest day; went to Clachnaharry to see Mr *[Thomas]* Jones *[probably the carpenter and lock-keeper for the Caledonian Canal]*.

October 5: Cold and wet; made several calls in the forenoon; dined at Dr Munro's to meet *[Rev.]* Mr Bethune of Dingwall.

October 6: Day very wet and chilly.

October 7: Ditto, ditto; engaged part of the day in tuning the organ.

October 8: Still very rainy.

October 9: As usual on Saturdays; made several calls and finished a sermon for Sunday.

October 10 (Sunday, 18 Trinity): Very wet day and rather thin Church; baptised a child at afternoon service. The Miss Edmunds dined with us (had hodgepodge *[a stew of odds and ends of food]* at dinner) for the last time.

October 11: A fine day. Miss Edmunds dined again. Mrs F. taken ill in the evening and obliged to go to bed – went to consult Dr Munro.

October 12: A fine day; at home most of the day, Mrs F. being confined to bed.

October 13: Mrs F. still confined to bed, but not worse; weather clear.

October 14: Mrs F. still in bed, but much better. A very showery disagreeable day. I dined at Ness Cottage and returned early. In the forenoon baptised Mr Shortt's child and made several professional calls.

October 15: Mrs F. continues better; a very fine day but the ground completely saturated with wet.

October 16: Much as usual on Saturdays; composed a sermon for Sunday on "the means of growth in grace"; pouring rain all day and very cold.

October 17 (Sunday, 19 Trinity): Wind and rain the whole day and consequently many kept from Church; there were 58 communicants. I preached in the morning and Mr Alves in the evening. At night it began to snow with heavy gale from south-east.

October 18: In the morning the ground quite covered with snow, which disappeared from the low part of the country as the day advanced.

October 19: Cold, wet and showery; dined at Kingsmills.

October 20: Rained incessantly till 5 o'clock, when there was snow.

October 21: Quite a snow storm, continued all day with little interruption.

October 22: Snow still lying on the ground in sunless spots; more than half the crops along the rising ground still in the fields. Mrs F. and I dined at Dr Munro's.

October 23: Another very dismal day, rain and sleet throughout;

occupied as usual on Saturdays, and in the evening Mrs F. and I dined at Mr Alexr. Robertson's to meet Mr and Mrs J. Ross, Rev. Mr Alves, etc.; came home early.

October 24 (Sunday, 20 Trinity): A perfect tempest of wind and rain; Church uncommonly thin. Mr Alves preached in the forenoon and I in the afternoon. Sir Ed*[ward]* Parry *[the naval officer, Arctic explorer and hydrographer, who had been appointed by the Government to make a personal enquiry about the usefulness of the Caledonian Canal]* attended both services – he appeared very devout.

October 25: Crossed the ferry to Redcastle where dined and staid all night; much interesting conversation with Mrs Baillie; met Mr and Mrs Fraser, Relig, Mr and Mrs John Mackenzie, Kinellan.

October 26: Spent the forenoon at Redcastle, and returned home about 5 o'clock – two very pleasant days and weather nearly fair.

October 27: Weather dry and cold.

October 28: Dry and frosty (nothing particular).

October 29: Frost and snow, ground hard all day and few potatoes out of the ground.

October 30: Thermometer 25°*[F; –4°C]* in the morning, no snow except in the hills, but otherwise like Christmas. Wrote sermon for Sunday on St. Peter's deliverance out of prison *[Acts xii.9]*.

October 31 (Sunday 21 Trinity): A mild, dull day; Chapel pretty full. Mr Alves read prayers morning and evening and I preached. Sermon on St. Peter's deliverance listened to with great attention.

November 1: A very beautiful day; the Miss Frasers, Ness Cottage, dined with us.

November 2: Another beautiful day; called at Kingsmills, Seabank, etc.

November 3: Bright and clear; people busily occupied in taking up their potatoes, and securing the remainder of their crops.

November 4: Weather still the same; called at Muirtown, etc.

November 5: Beautiful day; wrought for 2 hours with the boys in the garden, then went to town, where I was very, very sorry to hear of the sudden *[death]* of Mrs Shortt, whose child I had lately baptised. Reading "History of Port Royal" *[probably Port Royal des Champs, an abbey of Cistercian nuns south-west of Paris, established in 1204; the book cannot be specifically identified]*.

November 6; As usual on Saturdays; called for Mr Shortt, etc., etc.

November 7 (Sunday, 22 Trinity): A fine day and good congregation; at the conclusion of the sermon took occasion to allude to the death of Mrs Shortt.

November 8: Attended Mrs Shortt's funeral, and read the burial office at the grave in my surplice for the 2nd time at Inverness *[an influence of the Oxford Movement]*. In the evening Mrs F. and I and Charlie dined at Muirtown, the other two boys being at Ness Cottage.

November 9: A wet, disagreeable day; nothing particular.

November 10: Attended Infirmary committee, etc.; a wet, unpleasant day.

November 11: Weather wet and cold; dined at Dr Munro's; met a party.

November 12: Another similar day. News arrived of the birth of a male heir to the throne on the 9th *[the future King Edward VII]* .

November 13: Occupied as usual on Saturdays; day gloomy and wet.

November 14 (Sunday): Frost and snow; nothing particular in the services. Dd.*[?Donald]* Cameron, Polmaly, played the organ.

November 15: Frost and snow.

November 16: Ditto. Had a letter from Mr J. Mackenzie, banker, about Mrs xxxxxx.

November 17: Ditto.

November 18: Ditto. Had another letter from J. McK.

November 19: Ditto.

November 20: Ditto. Nothing occurred worth noting.

November 21 (Sunday, last Trinity): Frost and snow still continues; officiated with difficulty in consequence of a corn under the nail of one of my great toes. Announced collection for Church Episcopal Society *[probably Church Missionary Society]* for next Sunday.

November 22: Confined with sore foot.

November 23: Ditto.

November 24: Ditto. Frost and snow still continues; read Churton's "History of the Early English Church" *[Edward Churton, 1840]* and Paget's "Tales of the Village" *[Francis E. Paget, 1841]*.

November 25: Still confined to the house.

November 26: Able to go out a little; still frost and snow.

November 27: In town during the forenoon; attended practising; wrote a sermon for Church Society.

November 28 (Sunday, 1 Advent): Made collection for Church Society; sermon much admired; unfavourable weather, and collection only £15.

November 29: Soft gloomy day.

November 30: Day much the same; nothing particular.

December 1: Much the same every way; busy reading Englishman's*[?]* Library *[either 1st volume of "The Englishman's Library", in 31 volumes from 1840, or a book of that name published in 1824, edited by E. H. Locker]*.

December 2: Rain and mist; dark and dismal. Thanksgiving for the harvest.

December 3: Easterly wind, cold and cloudy. Walked to the ferry with Mr G. Anderson.

December 4: Wrote a sermon on "The Door Closed"; very dark, wet day.

December 5 (Sunday, 2 Advent): Dark, misty day; church pretty well filled notwithstanding; sermon much listened to and services good; had no clerk.

December 6: Weather much the same; nothing particular occurred.

December 7: Ditto, ditto; made several professional calls.

December 8: Ditto, ditto, ditto.

December 9: Spent most of the forenoon in walking and talking with Dr Munro chiefly about affairs and opinions at Oxford. Mrs F. and I and Johnny dined with him and remained till 11 o'clock.

December 10: Dark and rainy; nothing particular occurred.

December 11: Day dark and rainy, much as usual on Saturdays; received letters from Mr Bowdler, Mr Pratt, etc., etc.

December 12 (Sunday, 3 Advent): Nothing particular occurred; Church pretty well attended considering the day which was dark and rainy throughout. Dined in the afternoon with Mr G. Anderson to meet Applecross *[a Mackenzie]*.

December 13: Wet, dark and unpleasant day (reading much).

December 14: Do.;   do.   do.

December 15: Do.;   do. (visited Infirmary)   do.

December 16: Do.;   dined at Ness Cottage to take leave of Matilda and John before going south.

December 17: Frost and snow; busily occupied in reading, etc.

December 18: Much as usual on Saturdays.

December 19 (Sunday, 4 Advent): Very cold, dark day and Chapel rather thin. Mr D. Cameron played the organ and dined with us, Miss Howard also.

December 20: My birth day. Mrs F. confined with a cold.

December 21: Weather very severe and stormy; letters from Mr Copeland.

December 22: Ditto.

December 23: Partial thaw; called at Muirtown and attended pastoral duties.

December 24: Prayers in Chapel at 2 o'clock, etc., etc.

December 25: Exceedingly wet and unpleasant day, pouring rain and sleet – Church pretty full notwithstanding. 68 communicants; composed sermon for the day which was well listened to.

December 26 (Sunday, St. Stephen's Day): Day dark and slushy but Church very well attended notwithstanding.

December 27: Prayers in Chapel at half past 11; administered sacrament to sick persons.

December 28: Heavy rain most of the day; writing and reading busily.

December 29: Made several calls and did some business about Chapel.

December 30: Dark and dismal weather; nothing particular occurred.

December 31: Font put up in the Chapel – exceedingly well executed; variously occupied otherwise, and in the evening prepared for New Year's Day's service.

From the concluding portion of the Diary it is apparent that Dean Fyvie experienced a difficulty in keeping up his record of daily happenings. As can be seen, he was a very busy man, performing his varied and incessant duties in connection with his church with great fidelity. He also took an active part in looking after the poor, and was much interested in education and in the management of the Northern Infirmary. The Dean, as already mentioned, died in 1849, in his fifty-third year. In 1848 failing health necessitated the appointment of a colleague and successor, the Rev. Jas. Abereigh Mackay *[more correctly James Aberigh-Mackay]*, a native of Inverness, who for some years ably maintained the traditions of St. John's.

REV. JAMES ABERIGH-MACKAY, D.D.

Mr Mackay, who was born in 1821, was a son of Mr George Mackay, a well-known merchant and Presbyterian Church leader, first in the congregation of the Chapel of Ease (now the United Free East Church), secondly as one of the founders of the North Church in 1836, and subsequently of the Free High Church.

Rev. James Mackay laboured with much acceptance in St. John's till 1857, when

Rev. Aberigh-Mackay from a book illustration, dated 1897.

he was appointed an Army Chaplain in India, and went through the thrilling period of the Indian Mutiny. After his retirement from India he resided for a period in America, subsequently settling in Paris, and afterwards in the South of England. On the resignation of Bishop Low in 1851, it was generally expected that Mr Abereigh Mackay, as he had *[served in the Diocese]*, would be elected as his successor as Bishop of Moray and Ross, but contrary to expectation, Bishop Eden was appointed. The election caused strong feeling, and "from that time," says Miss Isabel Anderson, in her interesting sketch of St. John's congregation in "Inverness Before Railways," "the congregation of St. John's ceased to be a united one. Mr Mackay's supporters remained with him, while those who favoured Mr Eden gradually withdrew and formed a new congregation in the Mission Chapel." The two gentlemen lived to respect and admire each other.

Dr Abereigh Mackay died in Bournemouth in 1908. His eldest surviving son, Colonel James Livingston Abereigh Mackay, 8th Bengal Cavalry, was a popular Indian Army Officer, who died in 1920. The only surviving member of his family is [was in 1922] Lady Maxwell, who, in 1870, married Sir William Edward Maxwell, K.C., M.G., Governor of the Gold Coast during the Ashantee Expedition of 1896, who died in 1897.

The writer of this diary expressed the wish to be buried in the beautiful building erected mainly by his own exertions, but this was not to be. The Dean's remains rest in the Chapel Yard, in a grave alongside that of his father-in-law, Bishop Macfarlane, situated alongside the south [-west] wall, where is placed a stone indicating that the spot was the burial ground of three successive Episcopal clergymen, the Rev. James Hay, the Rt. Rev. Bishop Macfarlane of Ross and Moray, and the Very Rev. Charles Fyvie, Dean of Moray and Ross.

The graves in the Chapel Yard, Inverness, of Dean Fyvie (right – with cross) and Rev. James Hay, episcopal clergyman in Inverness from 1734 to 1758 (left). The wall plaque, marking the three episcopal clergy graves (including that of Bishop Macfarlane close by), is hidden by the hedge behind the graves.

Some 21st century comment:

The diaries of Dean Fyvie now of course belong to a former age, but tell us a lot about the Dean himself and to some extent his family and friends, his religious views (influenced by the Oxford Movement) and about Inverness and its politics in the first half of the nineteenth century. The Oxford Movement was a movement within the church arguing for the use of lost Christian traditions of faith and for them to be included into Anglican liturgy and theology. It is also known as the Tractarian Movement, named after a series of pamphlets, *Tracts for the Times*, published between 1833 and 1841, *i.e.* just at the time when Fyvie was active in Inverness.

Dean Fyvie was born on 20th December 1795, and attended Aberdeen University (King's College), graduating with an M.A. (then abbreviated as 'A.M.') in 1814. He became the family tutor to Sir Archibald Dunbar's family at Duffus, Morayshire, until he was ordained the following year. Fyvie became the incumbent at Duffus from 1815 until his move to Inverness in about 1819. His first marriage was to Jessie Adam of Westfield, Morayshire, born in 1796. The marriage took place in November 1820 in Duffus.

From a sketch by   [*Lydia Nicol.*

RUINS OF EPISCOPAL CHAPEL AND MANSE AT DUFFUS, MORAY: DEAN FYVIE'S FIRST CHARGE.

The couple probably had six children. In order of birth they were:

- Margaret (Maggie) Catherine, born at Clachnaharry on 1st November 1821. She married Arthur John Bowdler Godwyn in Gloucestershire in 1863, but her year of death has not been identified.

- Jessie Dunbar Fyvie, born on 28th January 1823, but died in June of that same year, aged only 5 months.

- John (Johnnie) Bell Fyvie, born 27th June 1824. He moved to lodgings in Old Aberdeen in October 1840 aged 16, when the usual age at that time for starting university was from about age 14 to age 16. He died in Australia on 31st August 1869, according to a death notice in a South Australian newspaper in September 1869, where it is claimed he was 39. This is clearly wrong, as he must have been 45.

- Charles Alexander Fyvie (a twin), born 11th March 1826, but died in May of that year, after only 10 weeks of life.

- James (Jamie) Robert Fyvie (a twin), born 11th March 1826. He apparently died in Australia in 1852.

- Charles (Charlie) Duff Fyvie, born 14th February 1828; he was possibly married in Hackney, London, in 1865, and may have died in Southern Africa in September 1868 (an on-line genealogical site shows two photographs of a gravestone there with his full name).

Dean Fyvie's first wife was to die only five months after the birth of her son Charles. Johnnie, Jamie and Charlie are listed in an on-line record of mid-nineteenth-century settlers in Natal, but it looks as if Johnnie and Jamie later moved on to Australia.[6]

The Dean's second marriage was to Miss Duff Macfarlane, the daughter of the late Bishop Andrew Macfarlane, on 3rd February 1830 in Elgin. Isabel Anderson, in her book, refers to

---

[6] The birth dates given here are taken from the Register of Baptisms, Marriages and Burials of St. John's Church, as are the dates of the death of both of the two children who died in their first year of life, and of the Dean's first wife. Other information about the family has been gleaned from a selection of websites, some of which provide inaccurate information.

Mrs Fyvie's favourite 'stepsons' living far away where the Dean's second wife could not look after them. After the Dean's death Mrs Fyvie moved to a house at the foot of Academy Street, where she continued to try to entertain friends. She became very feeble and was wheeled about the streets in a Bath chair by local boys who received some pennies in payment for this service.

The Dean's association with the poor and their education and welfare is noted with the survival in the Highland Council Archive of papers about the United Charities (see the diary references in January 1839 and March 1841). The United Charities were the Female Charity School, the Infant School and the Ladies' Female Work Society. In 1833 and 1834 Fyvie was trying to reduce costs and make their work more effective by combining the work of the three charities into one building. A printed proposal, probably dating from about mid-1833, has Fyvie's signature at the end of the text, but the space for the names of subscribers is blank. In early 1834 he appealed for support from the Town Council.[7]

The building (now a private house) at the top of Castle Street, at the divergence of Old Edinburgh Road from Culduthel Road, is still sometimes known as the United Charities Building. The modern official 'listed building' reference dates this building to 1836, but other references date the construction to 1840, so it may have been some years before the proposal came to fruition.

It is also a long way from the parts of the town (mainly to the north of the town centre) where the people who needed the services of charity schools would live. A petition, dated 1834, signed by 69 parents of children at the Infant School at the Thread Manufactory (near Douglas Place), stated that the proposed new school site was too far away from their homes, and it would be difficult and dangerous for children to go to it.

In the 1839 diary entry, it states that the sale of the United Charities buildings (in the plural) was underway. The 1841 diary entry indicates that the sale had been completed, suggesting that the move to the Old Edinburgh Road site had taken place by then. More work needs to be done to identify exactly where these charities were originally located in the town.

---

[7] Highland Council Archive (HCA), Ref. CI/5/27/6

A national report compiled in 1838 [8] provides details about the St. John's congregation. Membership was stated as being about 250, of whom about 120 were communicant members, with figures said to be on the increase. About 30 poor people formed part of the congregation. In summer between 200 and 300 attended services, but this fell to about 150 in winter. (This is not surprising as various landed families came in from many miles away by carriage to attend church.) There was seating for about 280. The income from seat rents was about £100, and a further £50 came from collections. Dean Fyvie's stipend was £180, but this did not include a house or glebe, although a small plot of land was available to him.

Many papers related to the building and opening of the 1839 St. John's Church still survive, and are held in the archives of the Diocese of Moray, Ross and Caithness.[9] Among the material are reports, bills and receipts for the building work, lists of subscribers, and correspondence. One of the more significant items is an 1843 report which lists the costs and income available for the chapel at that stage.

The costs included:

Site	£ 600
Building	£2716
Organ	£ 240
Miscellaneous	£ 330

making a total of almost £3900.

Income was very much less, and most of it had been obtained by subscription. The total subscriptions at that date were:

General	£2006
Organ	£ 143
Proceeds of sale	£ 122
Interest	£ 23

making a total of £2294.

Of the subscriptions, the largest part by far came from England with an anonymous donation of £600, together with subscriptions of £10 from both the Archbishop of York and the Archbishop of Canterbury. From the town of Inverness only

---

[8] From the Appendix to the Fourth Report of the Commissioners of Religious Instruction, Scotland, as quoted in: Strong, Rowan: *Episcopalianism in Nineteenth-century Scotland* (Oxford University Press, Oxford, 2002).

[9] National Register of Archives of Scotland (NRAS): Ref. NRAS4317/1/19, especially NRAS4317/1/19/4

£237 was raised, of which £50 came from Dr Munro. The rest of Scotland had contributed at that point £458.

A small amount of income came from a trust fund for lands at the Maggot which was later administered by the Town Council. The income was paid to the Episcopalian clergyman, but for the period covered by Fyvie's diary the rents do not seem to have been properly collected from people who were amongst the poorest in the town.[10]

The new building had seats for 600 people, with 100 of them available to the poor, without payment of a seat rent. This compared with the 280 seats in the previous church.

Clearly there was a major financial debt following the construction of the 1839 building, and this does not seem ever to have been cleared. Some of this debt was covered by the purchase of a bond, but at the time of Fyvie's resignation through ill health in 1848, an appeal was put out to members of the congregation and others for money even to secure a salary for his successor. A further appeal was made in 1866. In 1883 a major bazaar was held, with the 'great and the good' recruited as patrons and stall holders, but this met with limited financial success.

Part of the problem was that the Bishop's Mission Chapel (established by Bishop Eden) had opened in 1855, on the east bank of the River Ness, just south-east of where the Greig Street bridge is now located (probably on the site of the present Y.M.C.A. building). It was only about 200 yards from St. John's Chapel. As mentioned in the 1922 comment above, the St. John's congregation was split, with supporters of Bishop Eden gradually moving to the Mission Chapel. It had seats for 230, but closed when the Cathedral was opened for worship in 1869.

By 1900 a report on the St. John's building was commissioned from Ross and Macbeth (the firm of which Alexander Ross, architect for the Cathedral, was the key player). This report stated that, although the main frame of the church was sound, the lighter framing and plasterwork was moth-eaten and damaged, the skylights were leaking, the ventilation needed improving, and there was a need for a proper vestry and/or church hall.

A circular explaining the main options – major funding for repairs or combining with St. Columba's Mission (in a district

---

[10] Refs. NRAS4317/1/19/6 and HCA D845/2

then known are Barnhill, now part of the Crown area) – was issued in 1901, but the cost of the repairs was simply beyond the means of the diminished congregation. After various legal wrangles during 1902, which included argument in the First Division of the Court of Session on whether the Church had the power to sell the building and the land on which it stood, it was agreed to combine with the St. Columba's mission building in Southside Road, following extensions and modifications to that building. The plans for these changes survive.

In 1903 this created what we now know as St. John's Church in Southside Road. Various parts of the Church Street building were reused, such as the pews, the lectern, the organ and the font, with its wooden cover carved by a Mr Strachan, a cabinetmaker and church member.

The organ, originally built by Bruce in 1840, had been enlarged in 1889 by Wadsworth Brothers of Manchester (who had a workshop in Aberdeen), and some new stops were added. A further restoration took place in 1992, with work done by Harrison and Harrison of Durham, with further stops added. However the core of the instrument, including much of the upper casework and of the pipework, is still the work of Bruce from 1840.[11]

The Church Street site was sold, and for part of the second half of the twentieth century there was an auctioneer's business in the replacement building. In 2013 this is still recalled by the presence of a public house called "The Auctioneer" on the site of the former church. The original tower, built during the 1840's after the main building was completed, was not demolished until the 1950's.

Dean Fyvie's name is not well known in Inverness these days, but his legacy still survives through his diaries and other publications and writings. Also surviving are the bands he wore as a clergyman, which have been passed to the Diocese with a note as to their provenance.[12] Sadly we have no portrait of him.

---

[11] Information on the history of the organ has been supplied by Alan Buchan in a personal communication.

[12] Ref. NRAS4318/9

Appendix

A copy of the booklet of correspondence between Dean Fyvie and John Mackenzie, the banker, mentioned in Dean Fyvie's entry for 13 July 1839 as having being published, has been traced to Aberdeen University Library.[13] Thanks to help from the Library staff in locating the book it is possible to read about the details of the dispute. Today, reading the text becomes very tedious, but it is primarily about whether or not the land on which the 1801 chapel was built could be sold.

Mackenzie also claims that he should have been part of the committee discussing this, but that Fyvie had deliberately not informed him of meetings of the committee. The letters, which at times are written almost daily, start on 4th April 1839, and end on 26th June. Mackenzie concludes the pamphlet with a personal note, dated 5th July, claiming that such meetings as had been held were of subscribers to the new Chapel, and not of pew-holders in the existing one. He also claims to have had more information about the titles on the older building than anyone else. He says he had the support of the Bishop (Bishop Low) in his request for a meeting of pew-holders.

Mackenzie had been Provost of Inverness from 1833 to 1834, during which time he attended the Old High Church on Sundays, taking his place in the Magistrates' pew, even though he was an Episcopalian.

This dispute was at a time when there was beginning to be considerable discussion nationally in the Episcopal Church about the form of church government, and to what extent lay people, especially the middle-class, had a say in administration of the Church, a matter which only started to be resolved with the establishment of the Representative Church Council in 1876. However, during the 19th century, Bishops increasingly allowed lay involvement in the temporal management of the church, but it was not until much later that lay people influenced decisions on spiritual or doctrinal issues.

---

[13] *Correspondence betwixt John Mackenzie, Esq., Banker, Inverness, and the Revd. Charles Fyvie, relative to the Episcopal Chapel in Inverness*, published by R. Carruthers, Inverness, 1839.

Bibliography

Anderson, Isabel: *Inverness before Railways* (original edition: A. and W. Mackenzie, Inverness, 1885; reprinted by Charles Leakey, Inverness, 1984) (also available on-line)

Barron, James: *The Northern Highlands in the Nineteenth Century*, volumes 1 – 3 (especially volume 2: 1825–1841) (R. Carruthers and Sons, Inverness, 1903–1913) (also available on-line)

Bertie, David M.: *Scottish Episcopal Clergy, 1689–2000* (T. & T. Clark, Edinburgh, 2000)

Fraser, John: *Reminiscences of Inverness, its People and Places* (original edition: published by the author, 1905; reprinted by Charles Leakey, Inverness, 1983)

Scottish Episcopal Clergy information inserted in the diary text is taken from *Scottish Episcopal Clergy* by Bertie, with some corrections derived from other sources. Information about many of the other people mentioned in the diaries is taken from a large variety of easily-accessible websites.